Secrets

OF A
Baby Nurse

How to Have a Happy, Healthy,
and SLEEPING Baby from Birth

Marsha Podd, R.N.

Maternal-Infant Nurse and Lactation Specialist

iUniverse, Inc.
Bloomington

Secrets of a Baby Nurse
How to Have a Happy, Healthy, and SLEEPING Baby from Birth

iUniverse books may be ordered through booksellers or by contacting:

iUniverse
1663 Liberty Drive
Bloomington, IN 47403
www.iuniverse.com
1-800-Authors (1-800-288-4677)

ISBN: 978-1-4502-6164-7 (sc)
ISBN: 978-1-4502-6165-4 (dj)
ISBN: 978-1-4502-6166-1 (ebk)

Library of Congress Control Number: 2010914496

Printed in the United States of America

iUniverse rev. date: 12/08/2010

For my sister, Jennifer, who graciously allowed me to get to know and love each of her four children: Gregg, Anthony, Emilie, and Stuart. Each of them has given me bountiful knowledge that has enlightened my work with babies and honored me with the gift of a personal relationship that has touched my heart. Thank you, Jennifer, for sharing your children and your joy with me.

Contents

Preface

BABIES HAVE ALWAYS FASCINATED ME. Even when I was a young child, I loved to just watch babies. I observed their movements, the noises they made, and the way their mothers handled them. I watched their facial expressions and their body language. This helped me learn who they were. As a child, I practiced my own mothering skills by playing with dolls. My doll families were large and consumed all my attention. As I grew older, my focus turned to real babies. I began babysitting at a young age. It never felt like a "job" whenever I got to watch babies. I loved holding and playing with them and still consider it delightful to spend time with these fascinating souls. I earned a BS in child development, and later, after working in a medical clinic, I decided to return to school and complete my second degree in nursing. My specialty is in maternal and child nursing.

I welcomed my sister's four children into my life and also surrounded myself with babies from my own circle of friends. While I have no children of my own, I have been blessed with many close relationships with those who have shared theirs with me.

After a few years of working in two different large hospitals in Southern California and San Francisco, I ventured into running my own health and child-related businesses.

For more than ten years, I owned, operated, and taught at the Center for Creative Parenting in Northern California. It was there that I began to see the need for supporting new parents with my skill, education, and experience. While teaching groups for new mothers, I found the discussion would always turn to the topic of baby sleep and calming methods. Week after week, this was the favorite topic; thus, my research on infant and toddler sleep began.

Mothers began asking me to counsel them privately about their babies and sleep. Through word of mouth, my counseling business grew. More and more parents reached out for support. I realized that I wanted to share my wisdom so more parents could discover the joy of a well-rested, calm, and happy child. This critical need to educate parents about sleep has led me to write this book.

Mothers often refer to me as a "baby whisperer." A baby whisperer is a person with a special ability to intuit what a baby's needs are, and to help him or her be happy and calm. There are many "baby whisperers" on this planet of ours. I am only one of them. This book is based on research, personal study, and many years of experience, observation, and practice.

Most parents learn from just a few babies in their lives. I have been blessed with lessons from thousands. And now, I am excited to share my knowledge and experience with you. What you read here is amassed from many years of scientific research studies as well as my life's work, experience, and joy. I hope you can learn about your special baby by reading this book and, in practicing some of my techniques, create a calmer and happier relationship with your baby.

Support for a new parent is critical. If you find that after reading this material, you would like more in-depth information and a more personalized approach to your unique family and its needs, please seek help. Parents tell me it is well worth the investment. Since sleep and learning patterns are established early in life, learning about sleep and self-regulation can be invaluable to your child's future good health.

Acknowledgments

THANK YOU TO ALL OF the many friends and family who helped me with the completion of this book, both to those who responded to my e-mails with their comments and opinions, and to those who actually read the book and gave me feedback. I truly appreciate your giving spirits. If it were not for Cynthia Russell, Barbara Bowers, and my editor, Christopher McLachlan, I would never have completed this project. Your kindness and patience is woven into the pages of this book. Thank you for your diligence and endurance.

Thank you to my baby models, Erin (and mother Sara Dinnell), Graceann Skinner, Isabel Gray, Makayla Comino, Ania Vassileff, and Cole Kissell (and mother Emilie.) I especially want to acknowledge the photographer friends who helped me capture these precious babies in motion. I know the challenge of getting just the right photo. Thank you to Joy Padayhag ("Images of Joy," Sacramento, California) who contributed the cover photo, Carol Nelson of Paris, France, and Dan Kissell of Steamboat Springs, Colorado for contributing baby photos to this book. Also, thank you to Tami DeSellier of San Francisco for her back cover photo of me with baby Makayla Comino.

And finally, special thanks to all the thousands of mothers and babies in my life over the years who have helped me learn, study, and develop my wisdom and practices. I truly have been blessed in my life by the richness of meeting and holding so many thousands of new little souls.

Introduction

Parents often call me in a sleep-deprived state and beg me
to help them find the path to a full night's rest. I ask them if
they truly want to help their baby learn how to sleep better. It's
usually a tough job. Are they ready? This may be the first time
parents are confronted with letting go and letting their child learn
to self-soothe. It is an emotional process, and most parents find
it difficult. Sleep training represents the beginning of separation
between parent and child and therefore the beginning of more
independent lives.

I ask parents if they can be strong. Are they ready to cope with
some crying? They usually say, "We've tried lots of different sleep
methods and failed." They wonder where to begin. Their babies
are confused and fussy. Parents, from their own exhausted state,
are desperate. And they usually need lots of support, as they are
wounded from their past experiences. I promise them that if they
can persist for a few days to a few weeks, they will definitely see
a happier child and hear less crying.

This book is written with the intention of preventing the
wounded parent and the confused, unsure, and stressed child.
What follows is really a message from the babies (through me)

to you. They have taught me so much over the many years of my life. Pay close attention to what they need when they are young, and you too will create a happier, healthier, smarter, and well-rested baby.

On the Process of Letting Go and Letting Your Child Learn

The nine months it takes for a baby to prepare for birth while sheltered and nurtured in its mother's womb is a very special time. Life is vulnerable, and this new being needs to be protected. That is why a baby grows inside another person. Mother Nature is smart! At about thirty-seven to forty weeks of gestation, babies have developed enough physically (and emotionally) to be ready for survival outside of the mother's body.

Birth is the beginning of the separation between mother and child. The first phase usually takes twelve to twenty-four hours and a great deal of energy and focus. We celebrate with joy the severing of the umbilical cord and establishing a separate being. But separating mother from child is a long process, and it does not end with birth. On average, it takes fifteen to twenty years, or even more. Some never achieve complete separation. As humans, our task is to ready a child to live on his or her own. Ours is a complex and sophisticated world, and thus there are many requirements to learn for healthy survival. This can take years, so a child is safest with his or her parents until certain skills are developed.

Next to birth, the most difficult task a new parent faces is leaving the young child during the process of sleep. I see how parents struggle with letting go. It is probably more difficult for parents than for children. It is frightening to the new mother to leave her child and close her eyes. Since sleep sessions last longer and longer as the baby grows bigger, mothers have longer periods of separation from their babies. This leaves some mothers, especially during the first year of life, quite anxious. Both parent and child need to establish easy transitions, safe sleeping practices, and peaceful detachment. If you make wrong choices for you and your child at this time, it can have long-lasting consequences. Just as a pregnant mother enlists a childbirth educator to help her give birth, so should new parents seek professional help in later phases of the separation process when they struggle or have concerns.

If a parent's intention is to raise a child with her own values and behavior, the parent needs to consider fostering independence early. Think about this: Everything you do to help your child take care of herself and use her own set of skills (like walking and talking), makes her happier and more independent. Using her hands, crawling, rolling over, standing up, walking, running, riding a bicycle, swimming, and driving a car all help your child go faster, go farther, do more, and feel independent from you.

Every step your child takes away from you brings glee to his face. If your child is happy, you are happy. So, why not help him achieve these tasks of independence and help him reach his appropriate developmental goals? **Don't resist!** Parental resistance holds a child back. Such resistance can cause physical and emotional harm and poor psychological health. Choose to let your child take those first steps toward independence. Let him become his own person. Watching the development of your child is a very rewarding time in the life of your family.

Seek support when you run into difficulty. This is a tough job. Expert guidance will make it easier. Instead of experimenting, you will learn to guide your child appropriately. Letting go, and letting your child learn how to become separate from you is a long and involved process. It can be fun for everyone if you have a loving attitude. When you allow this separation, children will appreciate you even more because they will develop the life skills they need to survive without you. Be proud of accomplishing this difficult task.

Children become frustrated with this process as well. They need constant support and feedback from you that they are doing well and heading in the right direction. Your job as a parent is to provide safety and support as they continue to evolve. Your job is *not* to fix the frustration and remove the challenge. Frustration is a part of figuring things out. Frustration tolerance is a very essential life skill. It develops in infancy but continues to be with us all of our lives. If you don't let your child develop a bit of frustration tolerance, you will find that later she may not easily stick with a task in order to solve a problem but will rather be apt to give up easily and wait for your help and *your* solution. Imagine your child at age eight, attempting to solve a math problem, or trying to sit still and focus and learn. She needs to have some strength and practice in learning to tolerate the frustration until she can find the solution.

This process begins early. Putting your baby down to sleep is usually the first place parents feel this challenge of letting go and letting the child learn on his own. Your baby is very capable of learning self-soothing skills if you give him the opportunity. After the first few months, when you sense he has figured out who you are, you can start to practice. Be nearby, communicate as you go, and little by little you will see that your child really can put himself to sleep.

On Raising a Child in Modern America

When a baby arrives on planet Earth, she has no idea of our rhythms, night and day, or of sleep and activity. She lives on a twenty-four hour clock, her body programmed automatically by her mother's rhythms created during pregnancy. Cycles of feeding, activity, and quiet time have already been established in the womb and continue similarly outside the womb. A new baby's cycle does not match most adults' rhythms and routines. Pre-birth life is different than post-birth life. I think of it as wet-life versus dry-life. Just as land creatures behave differently than sea creatures, newborn babies behave differently than adults.

When a baby is born, the new parents' job is to teach him how to blend into our world and our rhythms. We are the teachers of his days and nights. We offer him times for activity, food, and sleep. While some adults do not seem to need a lot of certainty in their schedules, babies do. Babies feel stress if life is not predictable. Babies, who are non-verbal creatures, need to understand when to eat, rest, and have activity time, more so than adults.

Having been curious about these little creatures since I was a young child, I have learned how fascinating they can be. I have a good understanding of who they are by studying their desires and needs. If we lived in a culture where babies were worn (carried in a sling) next to their mother's body all day, the mother and child would learn each other's cycles quickly. Living in close company, they would perceive each other intimately. However, this kind of a culture fosters children who are extremely dependent on their parents. This is not a bad thing, but it is not the norm in America. In other cultures, family structures dictate dependence on each other.

Indigenous tribes in Africa are a perfect example of this. They need their families to help them survive. People in these cultures are dependent on the group rather than individuals to provide water, food, and shelter for the whole family. Families stay together for most of their lives and are very dependent on each other to maintain existence. In cultures where women do not wear their babies next to themselves (such as in the United States), mothers are not as aware of the baby's needs. The mother has to learn (often from books or friends) when the baby is most likely to need to eat, sleep, and be active. Role models may not be abundant as people live isolated lives, often distant from extended family. While fifty years ago parenting skills were passed down from parent to child, this is less likely to happen in today's world.

Recent studies and research in psychology and child development have created confusion among many about what is the "correct" parenting method for new mothers and fathers. There are many styles and choices. More than anywhere else in the world, Americans are a blend of many cultures, backgrounds, and past parenting experiences. Bringing all this past behavior and experience into the present can be challenging for today's new parent. In our society, where women have earned equal rights and, by choice or necessity, entered the workforce and now leave the home for extended periods just as men have always done, life has become more complex for the baby. Even in the past ten years, family life has changed tremendously. Parents are outsourcing much of their children's care to others, and thus "exact parenting" has recently come into play. I call it "exact parenting" because I find that the often older, more educated parent of today does not want to waste time experimenting on his or her children. They choose to go to experts for information and education. They do not want to go down the wrong path and suffer poor results. Older, wiser, and better read, they are linked to the latest research and advice on the Internet, and now need help implementing this advice in a quick and easy manner.

People in America want to lead active lifestyles and get out of the home more. Ironically, technology (instant communication) takes up more time; mothers do not spend as much time at home alone with their young children. In the U.S. we value independence and freedom. Consequently, our children have to adapt to our values. As mothers discover the activities and joy of their extended world, babies have no choice but to join them. Life is no longer quiet and mostly at home. Parents assume their children will enjoy the same rhythms as their own. This means flashing lights, loud music, computers, coffee groups, yoga classes, constant movement, and lots of activity and travel. As our world moves faster, so does theirs. This means the demands of the parents' world affect their baby's world as well. Mothers today do not realize the simplicity of the life of yesteryear.

Today's baby is often overstimulated with too much adrenaline and cortisol (hormones of alertness) pouring through his body's cells. He cries more frequently to burn off these stress-producing hormones. The fact is that many parents are overstimulating their babies, resulting in fussy babies who lack sleep. They can't sleep because they can't turn off the adrenaline in their bodies. This results in more crying and less sleep for everyone.

Prenatal research has proven that the emotions the mother feels while pregnant release hormones into her system. The baby is exposed to these *in utero*, sometimes resulting in unwanted consequences after birth. Depression in pregnancy can mean less sleep for the baby once she is born. The hormones the baby is exposed to in prenatal life affect her sleep cycles after birth. This is one of the many reasons why it is important to consult with a physician if you feel depressed while pregnant. Signs of depression may include chronic fatigue, not wanting to leave home, strange thoughts, and frequent crying.

Many mothers head home from work and stop to pick up their babies at the local daycare center late in the day. By the time Mom reaches home, it is 6:00 PM to 8:00 PM. Baby is tired.

He has had a stimulating day with lots of other children around him making noise and he has been exposed to electronic toys and flashing lights … you get the picture. He has taken a ride in the play saucer of fun, bounced in the jumper of delight, and has been exposed to the single dimension of a flat-screen television, as well as the electronic fields of cell phones and computers. He is fried by all the stimulation, just like his mommy and daddy. Because Mommy has worked all day (and Daddy, too), they want to play with their baby. Baby responds to the touch, tickles, and smiles. He is on hyper-drive, with extra cortisol in his body. He is active but quickly becomes fussy. Baby is actually craving quiet time. Parents are oblivious to the baby's needs and distracted by the fact that he wants to see Mommy and Daddy, too!

Thus, in response to this environment, the baby's body releases yet more hormones to take him to a still more alert state. Now he is wired and ready for action (for a short time). At 8:00 PM, when Mom and Dad are ready to call it a night, they put baby down in the crib and he wails loudly. Guilt drives the parents to pick baby up and take him to their bed where he is happier. All night long baby wants to engage with Mom and Dad and wakes often to touch and feel and maybe even feed. After a busy night, everyone is exhausted. Not much sleep is had by any. So, how do you get on the right path? How can we change this experience to a more healthy way of living? How can you help your baby become happier, more focused, and able to learn better? Read on. The answers are here within this book.

Chapter 1: In the Womb

Creating a Healthy Womb Environment

The approximately forty weeks a woman is pregnant is a special and transformative time. While some feel it goes by very slowly, it actually is almost too quick. In just nine months, parents are supposed to learn a lot about their child. There is much focus and support by the medical community and others on the process of pregnancy and birth, but very little on the several years of parenting that follow. In just a short nine months, one needs to learn about the care of a tiny newborn infant. It can be overwhelming if you are unprepared. We go to school for *years* to equip ourselves for a career, yet just nine months are given to parents to prepare their lives for the drastic changes that will come when the baby arrives. I have always wondered why, in one's teen years, there is more emphasis on learning to drive than learning to parent.

What a woman does while pregnant, and even prior to pregnancy, can affect the health and well-being of her child. Nutrition, chemical exposure, and a woman's emotional health can have an effect on her unborn baby. It amazes me to think that I, as an ovum (egg) in my mother's body, was affected by elements my grandmother was exposed to, such as chemicals, minerals, and toxins. My genetic material was once in my grandmother's body! Think about it. It's a little frightening, to say the least, for we have no control over the way our grandmothers behaved and the way they lived, yet the experiences and exposures of past generations can influence a fetus's well-being. More preparation and attention to physical and emotional health should be encouraged not only in schools, but also from the medical community. ***Before you get pregnant*** is the time to stop and consider your dietary habits, vitamin supplements, exercise, chemical and drug exposure, and lifestyle choices. The fetus will draw upon the resources of a woman's body and be affected by the life choices of its mother. Furthermore, many women make sacrifices while pregnant, but return to their old ways of behavior after the baby is born, forgetting that breast milk, too, is a living fluid with health benefits or dangers to the infant.

Believe it or not, a woman can affect her baby's sleeping ability right from the womb. Recent research out of Scandinavia has revealed the wonder of essential fatty acids to sleeping patterns. It has shown that pregnant women who eat a lot of fatty fish or take essential fatty acid supplements can increase the length and quality of their infant's sleep. Since the myelin sheath on a nerve fiber is affected positively by essential fatty acids, the fetus's nervous system benefits from being exposed to these nutrients.

Creating a calm and less stressful lifestyle can also benefit the womb environment. Women who consume lots of caffeine during pregnancy have jittery, hyperactive babies. The opposite is true as well. Women who remain happy and avoid depression while pregnant can have happier babies who sleep better. Women who attend to the health of their diets can have calmer babies. Avoiding hard drugs as well as certain prescription medications for the year before conception can have an impact on the health of the baby. It has been shown that, *in utero*, fetuses can be affected by loud noises as well as strong emotions, especially during the last trimester.

Mothers need to get adequate rest balanced with moderate activity for a healthy pregnancy. Pregnant mothers also need to avoid anger, grief and other strong emotions. Your medical doctor or other trained health professional can instruct you in a beneficial plan for you to implement prior to your pregnancy.

Rhythms of Life

Humans operate according to important rhythms of nature. They eat for energy, eliminate unneeded bulk and fluids, and must stay active to remain strong. They rest when tired. A typical day has repeated patterns of eating, activity, elimination, and rest. Babies also (even in the womb) repeat these familiar rhythms. When inside the womb, baby is most content and healthy when there is a natural rhythm to its twenty-four hour day. Mother Nature has created a rhythm that typically allows baby to be most active during mother's rest cycle. When mother is moving, baby sleeps, and when mother sleeps, baby is often active. When baby is born, she arrives on the planet with an opposite cycle to her mother's. A baby's most active time is usually when mother is sleeping or resting. I think Mother Nature created this rhythm on purpose, so that mother would pay closer attention to her infant at night when it is most vulnerable. For the first few months, a mother has to learn to attend to her alert baby during the darkness of night. Slowly, as she encourages baby to be more awake during the daytime hours, and baby achieves greater strength and activity, she learns to be more wakeful in the day and sleep longer at night. A parent's encouragement toward this daytime wakefulness is a necessary step in teaching baby a parent's natural rhythms. Thus,

I have found that both baby and mother do best if encouraged to begin a rhythm of feeding, changing diapers, having activity, and then swaddling and sleep right from the first days at home. It may take a month or two to see longer and longer stretches of sleep from your baby. Usually when baby is over ten pounds and at least two months old, the night sleep cycle approaches six hours of sleep at a time. I will discuss this pattern more fully in future chapters.

Setting up Baby's Sleep Environment

Prior to the arrival of your baby, it is important to look at the environment in which he will be sleeping. The Safe Sleep Campaign recommends that the baby be near his parents, but not in bed with them the first six months of life. Before the baby arrives is the time to study the sleep environment. Here are some questions to consider:

1. How much light is in the room on a scale of one to ten? (Ten being pitch black and one being light.) I recommend trying to create a room darkness that is an eight to ten on the scale.

2. How much noise will your baby be exposed to from the outer environment? Are there street noises, telephones, televisions, dogs or cats, or other children or family members in the same household? If so, I recommend that you invest in a good sound screen to block these potentially alarming noises and help your baby's brain relax. Low tone white noise can really improve sleep!

3. How dry is the climate? Your sleep environment is most comfortable and healthy between 40 and 50 percent humidity. Get a temperature-humidity gauge and see if you are in the healthy zone. Running a vaporizer or humidifier in the room for a few hours a day before sleep can improve humidity.

4. How warm do you keep the room? Most people are comfortable sleeping somewhere between sixty-eight and seventy-two degrees Fahrenheit. You may need to purchase a heater or air cooler if your room is very warm or very cool. Remember not to have too warm a room for baby to sleep in as it can place baby at higher risk for SIDS.

5. Do you or your partner snore? Are you restless sleepers who thrash around? If so, you *definitely* need a sound screen (my favorite is the SleepMate® 980A by Marpac).

6. Are there dim lights, blinking monitors, digital clock lights, or other lights facing your sleep area that could cause your brain to stay more alert? If so, cover them at night or turn them off. Use a small flashlight to maneuver in the dark.

7. Do you use aromatherapy for better, more relaxing sleep? Your local health food store can advise you which products are best. I recommend spritzing lavender water over the sleeping area, a natural antiviral, antibacterial agent and Mother Nature's mild tranquilizer.

8. How are you dressing your infant? Is she too cool or too warm? Do the clothes constrict her movement too much? Trust your intuition here and experiment to see if baby needs more or less layers of blankets and clothing. It is always better to put baby in a cooler room with more layers of clothing than in a room too warm for sleep.

In deciding where to put baby down to sleep, keep in mind the recommendations for safe sleeping: a firm, well-fitted crib mattress; no bumper pads around the crib or bassinet sides; no stuffed animals or other objects that can cause suffocation in the crib; and a quiet, toy free sleep space. In other words, make it a boring space so baby isn't amused in any way, thus creating the environment for sleeping soundly. And remember to only use blankets that are swaddled around your baby, never placed loosely on top of baby.

Some parents want to co-sleep with their baby. Pediatricians do not recommend it. If you nevertheless choose to do so, please be wise and place a firm and safe hard-sided bassinet between you and your partner to protect baby (there are many on the market).

My favorite is the Supreme Snuggle Nest® with Incline, which can be purchased online or in stores.

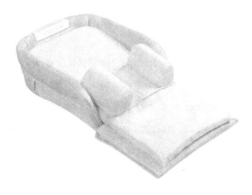

Fostering Family Wellness

Talk to your partner prior to your child's birth about your individual visions for comfort, quiet, and intimacy. Each person may have different expectations and it is important to discuss and compromise *prior* to baby's arrival. Many times, the arrival of a baby divides her parents' love because of lack of communication between the partners. Attention to individual needs is important to the survival of a marriage. Keep in mind that what works for one member of your family may not work for *all* members. Treat each person with respect. Consider his or her needs. Pay special attention to each other's sleep requirements. If one person is a light sleeper and can't sleep with the noises of a baby nearby, consider putting baby in a separate room. Your sleep environment and quantity of sleep is very important, as important as good nutrition. If you want your relationship to grow and be healthy, you must consider the needs of the other person whether or not they are *your* needs. Being able to make compromises *before* baby is born will bring parents together in a stronger and healthier way before baby arrives. If you can't resolve your conflicting needs, consider seeking a psychologist or mediator to counsel you and help you consider each other's differences in order make these important decisions in a way that feels equitable. Emotional well-being is every bit as important as physical health.

Preserve your relationship! Couples must remember that parenting can test the bonds of their partnership, and if you want it to stay strong and survive, you must pay close attention and cherish each other's needs as a priority. Do not let your new baby's arrival put your relationship at risk. Take some time to be alone with your partner each day (without baby in the room) to discuss each other's emotional needs. Work to be kind and not critical of each other. Praising each other's strengths instead of pointing out weaknesses can put you on a better path. Praise your partners when they step in and work with you. You need their support.

"Joey" or Why Create a Sedate Environment from the Start?

A local pediatrician referred a family to me with a three month-old baby who I will call "Joey." Joey was not eating well, and he wasn't gaining weight at a normal rate. He was fussy, and he cried every time Mom put him down. When I got to Joey's home, I sat down with the family and talked about him. I asked about the rhythms of his day and what was happening during his feedings. I uncovered a few important things. First, Joey had started out as a breastfed baby, but Mom quickly went to the bottle because she couldn't get him to nurse for more than a few minutes. Even with the bottle, Joey seemed to nibble and not want to drink much milk. Thus, Mom was feeding him constantly, all day long, trying to get enough milk into him for good growth. She was exhausted and Joey was actually being underfed.

Next, I noticed there was a lot going on in the home. The big-screen television was on constantly, blaring loud voices and flashing bright colors across the main living space where Mom and baby spent the majority of time. Joey was sometimes placed in the bouncy seat on the floor and Mom turned on the flashing lights on the play bar in front of him. The diaper-changing table had a music box that she wound up while Joey was being changed. It was all way too much noise, even for me. Joey, I discovered, was a very sensitive baby. He startled easily when Mom moved him from place to place. When we went upstairs to put him down for a nap, there was the sound of a babbling brook playing from a sound machine. Joey cried and cried. Normally, sound machines can work well at this age, but my intuition said to turn it off. As soon as I did, Joey was asleep in a few minutes. This is an example of how a very sensitive baby can be so bothered by what is going on around him that he is too stressed to eat and sleep.

As soon as we got Joey on a better schedule with some predictable quiet time and less stimulation, he did better. I also recommended that Mom try another formula, one that was lactose free and easier to digest. We changed the feedings to every three hours and I suggested she change the environment to be much more sedate. Joey flourished.

Knowing your baby's temperament can make a big difference in how you interact with him. While figuring out your baby and his needs can sometimes be challenging, experimenting with changes can be helpful. In this case, the mother learned that creating a quieter environment could produce a more soothed baby, one who could relax and eat.

Chapter 2: Your Newborn

Birth

After nine months of eager waiting, finally the baby arrives. But now what? When do you start reading and studying to become the best parent possible? What classes do you enroll in, and what books do you read? This is an awesome and overwhelming job. The truth is that parenting really begins when you get that first thought of becoming pregnant, the first gleam in your eye of your future child. You begin preparing for parenthood the moment you start thinking about raising children. Perhaps you have spent some time in therapy attempting to fix unhealthy family patterns. You might even have paid attention to what you ate and avoided unhealthy foods and drugs. You took care of creating a healthy womb environment at least a year before conception. This all prepared you for the beginning of your parenting path.

But the arrival of your child graduates you into a daunting role. What you do to set the framework in the first three years of your child's life will shape his future. Preparing in advance of conception by reading and studying is ideal, but unusual. Most parents stumble around with their first child and hope they make the right choices. Most people do not think ahead of their actions.

Ideally, you plan before you act. Thus, I encourage you to always prepare *before* your child reaches a new developmental stage. In other words, read about how you will deal with tantrums *before* your child is a one year-old. And read about toilet training *before* your child reaches age two. This way, you can give some thought to how to deal with these behaviors in advance of your child reaching each stage. This way you can actually avoid making lots of mistakes. The first three years of a baby's life are formative. You are laying a foundation for her future. What you do in these early years does matter. Most new mothers I have met welcome guidance. I tell them to think of the advice they read and hear from others just as they would visualize a huge library with lots of varying opinions. You must go inside yourself to determine if the information feels right. When you find what feels right, you can choose to apply it to your family system. There are more ways than just one to raise a happy, healthy child. Even your pediatrician's advice may not be a good fit for your culture and your family dynamics. Pediatricians have their own opinions and may guide you in a way that makes you feel uncomfortable. Know that it is okay to disagree with them. Trust your inner guidance. Follow your instincts. When unsure, seek advice from those you trust. And always follow safety standards.

While birth is an awesome experience, it can sometimes leave women unsure and emotionally tender. Having a confident adult whom you trust with you during this event can be soothing and a comfort. Consider having a doula at your child's birth. A doula is a person especially trained in supporting a woman through her birth experience. Doulas can also be helpful after birth. They can support and guide you as the first weeks of your baby's life begin. Sometimes a good friend or a sister, who herself has given birth, can perform this role. We know from collected statistics that women don't labor as long when a doula attends their baby's birth. Women also have fewer caesarean births when a doula is present during labor. While partners can be supportive, if this is your first child, I highly recommend having a separate person to support *both* of you through the transition of birth and into parenting, as both mother and partner need guidance and encouragement in this transformative eventful process.

Since many couples live far from their extended families, it is not always easy to have help and support as you adjust to being a new parent. One of the most important tips I can give you is to invest in setting up your life the first weeks after the baby arrives so you have support and physical comfort as you adjust to the new rhythms and routines brought on by a new baby.

Transitioning to Home

Bringing baby home from the hospital or birth center is always an exciting day. It can also be a bit overwhelming and frightening. Some people like to have support from friends and relatives, and others like the quiet solitude an empty home brings. Beforehand, think about what you feel would most nourish your emotions. Talk to your friends and family *in advance* of your baby's arrival about your vision for the first days at home. Discuss with your partner how to handle unwelcome guests. Cherish your chosen path and set limits. Putting a message on your phone's voicemail about your baby's birth (weight and sex, etc.) can help limit the traffic. Ask your partner about perhaps e-mailing a photo to friends and family with a friendly reminder that you are resting and healing and need quiet time before allowing visitors to meet your new addition to the family. You might want to print out a newborn photo of your baby and tape it to the front door with a sign saying that you are resting and not yet up to having company.

That way your friends and neighbors can see the baby and wait more patiently until you are ready for a visit.

Whatever you decide, just remember that the first day home with a new baby is a transition and you will want to allow plenty of time to settle yourself and your baby into this new environment and routine. Allow abundant rest and sleep time for the new family. It is my experience that babies tend to sleep a lot this first day home and then are up a lot the first night. Prepare yourself for a busy first night home. Most newborns want to eat every hour and often fuss with gas or needing to burp. When you are a sleep-deprived parent, the night can feel endless. It helps to be emotionally prepared for this.

By the time day two begins at home, you may decide that it might not be such a bad idea to have a few extra helpers around. New babies like to be held a lot; just getting a shower can be difficult. At first, newborns do like to sleep a great deal during the day, so plan to take daytime naps when the baby is napping to recharge yourself. Also, plan to have several small meals and prepared foods handy, as you may only get ten minutes to eat between taking care of your baby and trying to get some rest. Let friends make meals! Just ask them to call first and drop food off with a very brief visit. When friends ask to help, don't turn them down. People like to feel helpful and you will appreciate this service. Eat, sleep, and cuddle your baby. Nest, nourish, and recover. Begin to get into a rhythm with these cycles of eating, sleeping, and being active so your baby can learn about life on planet Earth. During the day, feed baby, then after about ten minutes of holding and burping her, change the diaper (which will awaken her). Play with your baby (at least fifteen minutes after each feeding), then swaddle her and hold or bounce her until she is asleep. Then, you can go to sleep, eat, or shower for the one to two hours your baby is sleeping. If you follow this routine all day long, in a few days she will understand when to awaken and when to sleep and life will be more pleasant for both of you.

Staying Sane

One of the best ways to maintain sanity in your life is to have some predictability and understanding about your daily rhythms around sleep and food. If you know when your meal times will be and when your free time will be, you can relax and enjoy life. This is true for baby, too. Consistency is very important to creating success in having a calm child. It is not about what *time* you feed your baby, but about the patterns and the order in which you link your daily tasks in caring for the baby that are important. At first, just think of a cycle as about a two to three hour period of time. During each cycle your baby will need to be changed, have some food, be held, amused and touched with the opportunity to stretch and kick, and will want some sleep. From the first day home, you can create this pattern: **feed, change diaper, play, swaddle** and finally, **sleep.** When baby awakens, you repeat the same cycle of feeding, changing the diaper, activity or play, then sleep time. Let's talk a little about each part of this cycle so you can understand how they fit together into a rhythm. But before we begin, I want to tell you about a special form of baby communication.

The Fuel Gauge

Wouldn't it be helpful to parents if baby came with a fuel gauge just like our automobiles have? Then we would know when to keep encouraging baby to feed appropriately. If only it were so easy. As a nurse, I have noticed that babies do have fuel gauges!

The Fuel Gauge

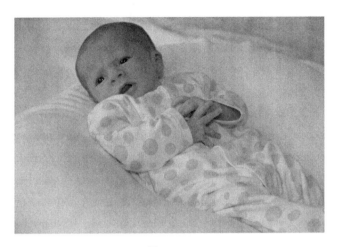

Empty

When arms are flexed, baby is hungry.

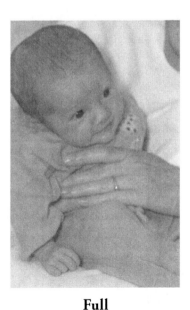

Full

When arms are straight and relaxed,
eyes open after a feeding, baby is full.

Their crying, as well as the placement of their arms, act as signals parents can observe. Notice when baby is hungry, how his arms and hands are right by his mouth? Stiff and unable to be bent straight, the arms are ready to massage the breast for milk, or hold the bottle. This arm signal says baby is very hungry. Please feed.

When baby has finished eating, is awake, and happy with a full stomach, her arms are straight, limp, and very relaxed. You will notice this when burping her. During the day, make sure you *always* wake baby up after feeding is over, and check her fuel gauge with her eyes *open*. If you read her arms as relaxed, and baby appears happy, then you can stop feeding her and move into a diaper change and then activity time (except at night). However, this sign may not be appropriate for babies born prematurely, so if your baby was born before thirty-seven weeks, please don't fully trust this fuel gauge sign as accurate, since premature babies are more relaxed due to their immature development.

Initiating the Cycle—Feeding

Feeding time is when to think about *your* food intake and nourishment and then your baby's needs. If you are a breastfeeding mother, make sure you have had something to eat and drink in the past few hours. If you haven't eaten, take a few minutes to restore your energy by grabbing a snack or meal. Make sure you drink plenty of water! If your baby is between six and eight pounds, like most newborns, he will need about two ounces of milk each feeding. If breastfeeding, you can't measure this, but you can look at certain signs that will tell you if your milk supply is adequate. If your baby is three to five days old, your milk should be in and you should see the following signs:

- *At least* four to six wet diapers in a twenty-four-hour period.

- *At least* a few bowel movements that are starting to change from black to green and then to a yellow color (watery is normal).

- A hungry baby who wants to eat about every two to three hours (more frequently means he may be getting only scant meals).

- You hear good swallows and gulps for five to ten minutes at each feeding on each breast.

- Baby looks relaxed, content, and happy. You can tell by gently waking him up while burping him to see if his arms are hanging loosely after feeding. If his arms are flexed and he is fussy, he hasn't had enough to eat. As you learned in the last section, these arms are like a fuel gauge. When flexed, baby is hungry. When straight, baby is full.

Your baby should be able to be awake and still look content and happy (not crying). I recommend that in the daytime you awaken baby after each feeding to make sure she has fed enough and is satisfied. I have known too many parents who just feed baby to sleep and put her down. Sometimes, when babies are first born, they do not awaken when hungry. This can lead to a baby who doesn't gain weight normally or becomes lethargic. Make sure your baby has eaten really well. Awakening her is a test to see how content she is after feeding. It also establishes the pattern of waking up after feeding and having activity. Then your child learns to fall asleep when tired, after activity, not just because her stomach is full. This is a healthy way to establish good rhythms early in life.

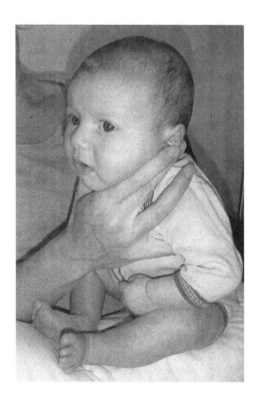

Make sure to burp baby well after his feeding. This is best done by sitting baby on your lap and supporting his jaw with one hand and his upper body with the other while patting his back above the waist. If baby doesn't burp after a few minutes, gently move him around a bit in a small circle while supporting him in this upright position. Spend five minutes burping baby at the end of feeding time, and at least two minutes burping him halfway through the feeding. Don't worry if you don't get a burp. Not all babies need to burp with each feeding. It is helpful to keep baby's head above his stomach for at least thirty minutes after feedings to ensure that the air in the stomach rises and escapes. Most newborns are not happy when set flat after a feeding, as their stomach muscles can be weak and they can experience discomfort with milk or acid, or air regurgitating into their throat. That is why many babies complain when you set them down in their cribs after a feeding. Some babies are comfortable only when their heads are elevated. In this case, you may want to purchase a wedge to put in the crib or sleeping space to allow your baby to be kept at an incline. I believe baby is safer sleeping when his head is elevated slightly. Usually about a four- to six-inch elevation is sufficient. In fact, young babies under three months do not really like being on their backs unless they are swaddled and slightly upright. The photo below is an example of an incline wedge, which can be used in the crib or bassinet. Check with your doctor to see if it is appropriate for your baby before using one.

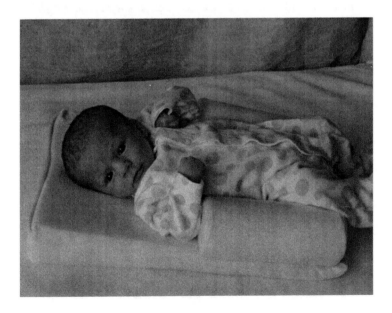

Diaper Changing

After each daytime feeding, check to see if your baby needs a new diaper. She should have at least four to six wet diapers from day four to day seven, then more like six to eight wet diapers after one week of age. Stools should be changing color toward yellow (if breastfed) or brown (if formula fed). If your baby doesn't have any stools for two to three days, please check with her doctor to see if there is a problem and reason for concern. This can also be a sign of low mother's milk if breastfeeding. It is best to wash your baby's skin well (diaper area) once a day with running water. Try to avoid the use of diaper wipes the first month, if possible, since baby's skin is so new and fragile. Some babies cannot tolerate the chemicals used to preserve diaper wipes and will get red skin from them or a rash. Wet some soft paper towels (I like Viva®) and put them in a closed container by the changing table to make your own diaper wipes.

Putting your baby naked in the sunlight by a *closed* window in your house for about ten minutes a day can also keep baby's skin healthy and rash free. Remember, **no direct sunlight** (we want to avoid sunburn).

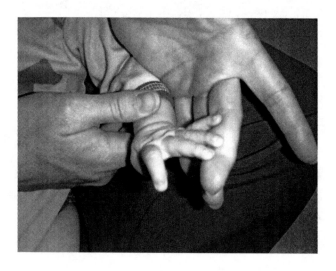

Be sure to check baby's fingers and toes daily. Your hair can easily become entangled in them and cut off circulation.

Playing

The time for baby to be awake should be after he has fed well and has been burped and changed. Expect at least fifteen minutes of awake time from your baby the first few weeks *after* each feeding. This awake time will lengthen as baby gets bigger and older. When he is under three months, he can only cope with about an hour of awake time with each feeding cycle. If you push him beyond this, it can result in a grouchy, overly tired infant. Try to keep life fairly quiet for your baby. Taking him out into noisy environments can make him fussier and it will be harder for him to get to sleep easily.

If your baby resists waking up and can't keep her eyes open, briskly rub her back with your hand or walk your fingers up and down her spine, move her back and forth, take her clothes off, or clean her face with a cool, wet washcloth to keep her alert. Just touching and talking to her (even with her eyes closed) can be stimulating to her, so don't worry if each and every time she doesn't fully wake up. Usually the diaper change will awaken her, but not always. If your baby is jaundiced, or extra sleepy due to Mom's use of pain medication, it may take some extra effort to awaken her. If you can't easily awaken her and she won't eat for more than six hours, please notify your baby's doctor, as this might be a sign of illness. Remember, it is important for newborns to eat about every two to three hours around the clock. A big baby over nine pounds may eat more and go a four or five hour stretch, but even these big babies need to eat about every four hours. If your baby won't eat this frequently, please consult your doctor.

During playtime, expose your infant to highly stimulating patterns of black and white. You can find some great patterns on the web at www.zorger.com. Remember, just talking to your baby, having skin contact, and touching him may be enough for him the first week he is home. Do what feels comfortable to you. The idea is not to stress your baby (or you), but to try to create some healthy awake time and activity cycles, with eyes open. By week two, he should respond more easily when you attempt to arouse him.

Swaddling and Sleeping

When newborns are tired, they generally just close their eyes and go to sleep. However, the first few days home, if you are a breastfeeding mom, your baby may only be getting small amounts of colostrum or breast milk. He might be on the hungry side. This is normal and it is Mother Nature's way of making a hungry baby who wants to nurse often, thus stimulating your hormones to help create a good milk supply. So, during this transition time, nurse your baby as much as he likes. After about fifteen minutes of awake time (talking and touching baby), you may decide to go ahead and swaddle your baby (see how to swaddle your baby properly in Chapter 3). This snug wrapping of a blanket around him is a familiar feeling and helps to center his energy and calm him. It becomes a signal to baby to quiet down and go to sleep. Some babies will just close their eyes and fall asleep. Others may fuss a bit. It is fine to gently bounce your baby up and down to help lull him to sleep. Once asleep, get in the habit of putting baby in his sleeping place in a quiet and dark room. Generally, most newborns will do a lot of sleeping the first two weeks at home, so expect a one to two hour nap before he awakens and wants to eat again. Use this time to rest, eat, and do your daily activities. This pattern will become more predictable with time.

More on Breastfeeding

Once you see your baby more satisfied, hear big gulps, and see milk in her mouth, you know things are improving. It may take as long as two weeks to build your supply to an adequately abundant amount. If you sense your breast milk is low after three to five days, you may need the advice of a lactation consultant or your physician to build up your milk supply. Using a breast pump to stimulate and also assess the quantity of milk you are producing can be helpful. Some women have plenty of breast milk, but baby may not be getting the milk in appropriate amounts at each feeding. Women with large nipples can have this problem as some babies just can't get enough of the areola in their mouths to empty the milk sinuses underneath. Use your intuition to judge whether your baby is feeding well.

Again, in the first few weeks, watch your baby's weight carefully. Get a weight check a day or two after leaving the hospital (from a home visit nurse or at your doctor's office) and again at least one more time one to three days after this. Then you will have a good idea of how you are doing with the feedings and about your baby's growth and well-being.

Formula Feeding

Some small or premature babies just don't have great sucking ability and strength and may tire easily and thus not eat well, even from a bottle. They can fool you. They may look like they are sucking and swallowing, but they may not be getting adequate amounts. Also, some babies may have a short, tight membrane on their tongue (frenulum) that hinders good sucking strides and thus will produce a weak suck. If you think your baby isn't eating enough, please seek your doctor's advice about extra feedings by bottle, cup, or spoon. Most newborns will need about one to two ounces of formula or breast milk every two to three hours. Large babies (over eight pounds) may take two to three ounces at a time. Your doctor or a lactation specialist can help you decide how much is appropriate for your baby. Some babies don't do well with formula, an artificial milk; watch for signs that may indicate this. Vomiting, crying a lot, a rash around the mouth, or body stiffness and fussiness can all indicate a problem. Some babies need specialized formulas or hypoallergenic formulas. Be extra watchful if you have allergies in your family. It is always ideal if baby can have just breast milk the first few weeks, but this is not always possible due to the low milk supply of some mothers. Be attentive to assessing your baby's milk consumption.

"Madison" or Building a Manageable Structure

A mother contacted me to say she was feeling overwhelmed and out of control as well as sleep deprived. Her doctor suggested she call and get some help organizing her schedule to allow her to have some time "off" from the children as well as be able to get a good night's rest. Her second baby, "Madison," was just ten weeks old. This was a breastfeeding mother of two young children. Her older son was just over two years old. We began by discussing their family routines, feeding schedules, sleeping environment, and active lifestyle. I gathered a lot of important information, the most obvious being how fast paced their lives were.

This family shared an active, full lifestyle. They were used to being outside doing things in their beautiful lakeside hometown. They belonged to many groups and often had dinner at friend's homes or in restaurants. Their two-year-old was involved in three different gym, music, and craft classes. This is very typical of today's family. The only time parents seem to keep children at home is in the first few hours of the day. Then, parents today tend to leave their home to connect with others and create fun and stimulation.

When you have a young baby who requires four or five naps a day it is difficult to be on the move and also instill good sleeping habits. When you are so active that your baby is always sleeping in the car or stroller, or when you are carrying her in a baby pack, she learns to need motion to fall asleep. This will become an obstacle to good sleep and it is a poor program for learning how to fall asleep and stay asleep.

Not only are you demanding a lot from young children, but you are also asking a lot from yourself when you are too active. It is important to get out of your house each day, but make it for only a few hours each day or you will exhaust yourself. This family was overbooked, and they had their children in the car moving from place to place a lot each day.

As I pointed out these things to Madison's mother, she began to understand that she needed to create more home time while her baby was still so young. She was so tired and overwhelmed that she craved this time at home, but she didn't realize it until we talked about her family's sleep issues.

I explained how important it was for her emotionally and spiritually to get out of her house each day and connect with other mothers and young children. I encouraged her to arrange play dates for her older son in the morning so he could go to a neighbor's house or another child could come to their house to play. I told her to arrange her time away from home either later in the morning or afternoon; that way she could plan her time more easily and fit in a nap for herself as well.

I also explained how important it is to take some alone time for herself to replenish her energy and spirit. She could trade off babysitting with another family during the daytime, or use her evening time when dad was at home to watch the children.

"Playtime outside with the children is important as well," I told her. Sunlight and fresh air help you and your children sleep better. As you expose yourself to the natural light of the day, the body produces melatonin, which, as it increases, encourages sleep. Plan outdoor time every day for at least an hour (remember to use sunscreen, and keep baby covered up for protection). Everyone benefits from exercise and natural light.

We also discussed some activities that her older son could do while her hands were full with baby. Crafts, such as stickers, crayons, or play dough can entertain toddlers well. Keeping some small toys or craft items in a small box and rotating boxes daily can help so your child doesn't get bored. Try to keep a similar activity plan daily so your toddler will learn to trust this consistent schedule. As a toddler learns to gain independence, he craves consistency and wants predictability in his life.

Slowing life down and making it less stimulating can help your children remain more calm and interactive. "Don't over schedule your life," I told this new mother. The other activities can wait until baby is over six months of age. As children learn good sleep habits, parents get more sleep and then everyone has more energy. We outlined a good rhythm for their day, and as we did so, I could see this mother start to relax. She thanked me for giving them more time to be at home to relax and establish a good nap schedule for the children.

Chapter 3: The Basics

The Sleep Plan Begins

You can begin to shape your child's sleep behavior from the first week. Tuning into your baby's needs and temperament will help you start to figure each other out. The rhythm of feeding upon baby's awakening, followed by a diaper change, an activity, then swaddling and sleep will set the pace for a good future. Your baby will learn this rhythm in about forty-eight hours. He will start to understand his world and begin to know what to expect. This is the rhythm for daytime. As your baby gets older, his activity time should lengthen to about sixty to ninety minutes. Since babies eat about every three hours, each cycle from feeding to feeding should include about ninety minutes of awake time, and about ninety minutes of sleeping or quiet time. Some babies eat quickly and others eat slowly. Some babies have sensitive tummies, spit up easily, and can't eat too much at a time. You need to be sensitive to your baby's individual needs. He may be in a two-hour cycle of feeding or in a four-hour cycle. Whatever the time frame, try not to let your baby sleep more than about two hours at a time during the daylight hours. When naps are longer than two hours, it lengthens the feeding cycle. As a result, some babies don't get enough food and activity during the day and this can interrupt sleep at night.

For the night, you will want to teach your baby how to be quiet and calm. Thus, keep the room dark and try not to talk to baby at night. Turn on only a small light during feeding time. Don't keep a night-light glowing in the room all night. Ideally, if you can keep baby swaddled during feeding, she will fall back to sleep quickly after eating and then so can you. If you must change a diaper at night, do so at the halfway mark in her feeding time. Diaper changes really can awaken a baby and then you will likely have a rough night with a wakeful child. Putting on a larger diaper for nighttime sleep can make baby more comfortable.

I usually advise parents to hold in mind the framework of the pattern they are trying to reinforce during the night. When a baby is less than ten pounds, he can only sleep for about a four-hour stretch without needing food. For these babies, don't change the diaper for four hours. When baby is twelve pounds, he is able to go a six-hour stretch without food, so don't change his diaper for six hours. And when a baby is fourteen pounds, he is able to sleep eight to twelve hours without feeding, so no diaper change all night. When you start to treat baby quietly and hold this concept, he will begin to rest better and be less wakeful and you will get longer sleep periods.

Many parents tell me that their babies are uncomfortable in a wet or dirty diaper. I disagree. I have never met a baby for which this held true. I think it is more *our* issue than theirs. We don't like the smell. Have you ever seen an older baby who just *loved* to get her diaper changed so much that she asked you to change her or willingly cooperated for the diaper change? I doubt it. Just try this plan and see what happens. Mothers' feedback over my years of practice is that this No Diaper Change Plan really helps keep baby quiet longer at night. Until your baby is over twelve pounds, all you should focus on is setting up good rhythms to day and night.

Sleep Cues

In order for a baby to sleep all night, he must learn how to self-soothe. If a baby learns to fall asleep without your help in his first year of life, he will have acquired techniques for future self-calming. What a baby learns about the falling to sleep process is the key to healthy sleep habits. If your involvement is needed to get your baby to sleep (such as rocking or patting him) beyond three months, then your child will have difficulty learning to become a good sleeper. He will depend on your presence to return to a state of sleep and will call for you by crying every hour or two all night long. Whenever someone interacts with him in the process of his going to sleep, it creates dependency for that rhythm each time he awakens. When a baby is under three months of age and is in the "inward" developmental phase, he is not aware of what you are doing to help him fall asleep. If baby is bounced, rocked, sung to, swaddled or held, it doesn't seem to have great impact on his future sleep habits. He still perceives himself to be part of Mom. He doesn't feel separate from her. Thus, I see no big problem with using these tools to help put baby to sleep if he is under three months old. Please try not to overuse them. Around three to four months of age, when a baby begins to show signs of independence—using his hands, arms, and legs—it is a cue to the parent to start letting go, and let baby learn, on his own, the art of falling to sleep.

Babies love predictability, as it gives them a sense of their world and what to expect. Repeating a customary pattern prior to putting baby in her bed is a good idea. A five to fifteen minute routine that includes dressing, massage, cuddling, reading, soft talk, and singing or music is healthy. Include this transition each time, whether naptime or bedtime, so your baby will learn the cues. I like to pull the blinds shut, turn off the lights, say "nighty-night" to all the child's toys, cuddle and rock her a few minutes, softly sing a short lullaby to her, and then put her in her bed, keeping my hand on her tummy for just a few seconds, then leaving the room. Usually parents offer a short version of this transition time for naps, and a longer version for nighttime.

Expect that baby will cry when you walk away from him, especially at first, for he does not want you to leave, nor does he want to disconnect from the exciting world around him. As he gets used to the routine, and if you have a well-rested baby, eventually you should have no crying or just a few minutes of protest. The type of crying and the length will depend on the temperament of your child and the timing of the sleep session, how early in the day it is, and how well rested your baby is. The difficult part for some parents is making peace with this transition time.

Safe Sleep

One of the most important things to consider when putting baby down to sleep is that she remains safe in her sleep environment. Parents need to feel certain that when they walk away from the crib, nothing can possibly happen to baby to cause her to stop breathing. A safe crib environment is essential. Here are the safe sleeping recommendations from the American Academy of Pediatrics:

- Back to sleep: Infants should be placed for sleep in a supine position (wholly on the back) for every sleep time, day and night. Side sleeping is not as safe as supine sleeping and is not advised.

- Use a firm sleep surface. A firm crib mattress, covered by a sheet, is the recommended sleeping surface, nothing else.

- Keep soft objects and loose bedding out of the crib. *Never* put soft objects such as pillows, quilts, comforters, sheepskins, and stuffed toys in an infant's sleeping environment and they should *never* be placed under him. If bumper pads are used in cribs, they should be thin, firm, well secured, and not "pillow-like." In addition, loose bedding such as blankets and sheets may be hazardous. If you are using blankets, they should be tucked in around the crib mattress so that the infant's face is less likely to become covered by them. One strategy is to make up the bedding so that the infant's feet are able to reach the foot of the crib, with the blankets tucked in around the crib mattress and reaching only to the level of the baby's chest. Another strategy is to use sleep clothing with no other covering over him, or infant sleep sacks that are designed to keep him warm without the possibility of covering his head.

- Do not smoke during pregnancy. Maternal smoking during pregnancy has emerged as a major risk factor in almost every epidemiologic study of SIDS (Sudden Infant Death Syndrome). Smoke in the infant's environment after birth has emerged as a separate risk factor in a few studies, although separating this variable from maternal smoking before birth is problematic. Avoiding exposing an infant to second-hand smoke is advisable for numerous reasons in addition to SIDS risk.

- A separate but proximate sleeping environment is recommended. The risk of SIDS is reduced when the infant sleeps in the same room as the mother. A crib, bassinet, or cradle that conforms to the safety standards of the Consumer Product Safety Commission and ASTM (formerly the American Society for Testing and Materials) is recommended. "Co-sleepers" (infant beds that attach to the mother's bed) provide easy access to the infant, especially for breastfeeding, but safety standards for these devices have not yet been established by the Consumer Product Safety Commission. Although bed sharing rates are increasing in the United States for a number of reasons, including facilitation of breastfeeding, the evidence is growing that bed sharing, as practiced in the United States and other Western countries, is more hazardous than having the infant sleep on a separate sleep surface. Therefore, it is recommended that infants not bed share during sleep. Infants may be brought into bed for nursing or comforting but should be returned to their own cribs or bassinets when the parent is ready to return to sleep. The infant should not be brought into bed when the parent is excessively tired or using medications or substances that could impair his or her alertness. The infant's crib or bassinet can be placed in the parents' bedroom and located close to their bed, which will allow for more convenient breastfeeding and contact. Infants should not bed share with other children. It is very dangerous to sleep with an infant on a couch or armchair.

- Consider offering a pacifier at naptime and bedtime. Although the mechanism is not known, the reduced risk of SIDS associated with pacifier use during sleep is compelling. Until evidence dictates otherwise, use a pacifier throughout the first year of life according to the following procedures.

  1. The pacifier should be used when placing the infant down for sleep and not reinserted once she falls asleep. If the infant refuses the pacifier, she should not be forced to take it.

  2. Pacifiers should not be coated in any sweet solution.

  3. Pacifiers should be cleaned often and replaced regularly. For breastfed infants, delay pacifier introduction until one month of age to ensure that breastfeeding is firmly established.

- Avoid overheating: The infant should be lightly clothed for sleep, and the bedroom temperature should be kept comfortable (sixty-eight to seventy-two degrees). Over-bundling should be avoided and the infant should not feel hot to the touch or sweaty.

- Avoid commercial devices marketed to reduce the risk of SIDS. Although various devices have been developed to maintain sleep position or to reduce the risk of rebreathing, none have been tested sufficiently to show efficacy or safety.

- Do not use home monitors as a strategy to reduce the risk of SIDS. Electronic respiratory and cardiac monitors are available to detect cardio respiratory arrest and may be of value for home monitoring of selected infants who are deemed to have extreme cardio respiratory instability. However, there is no evidence that use of such home monitors decrease the incidence of SIDS. Furthermore, there is no evidence that in-hospital respiratory or cardiac monitoring can identify infants at increased risk of SIDS.

- Encourage "tummy time" when the infant is awake and observed. This will enhance motor development, and a strong baby is a safer sleeper.

Follow these recommendations to both increase safety and to help prevent positional plagiocephaly (a deformity of the skull):

1. Avoid having the infant spend excessive time in car-seat carriers and bouncers, which apply pressure to the occiput (the back of the skull). Upright "cuddle time" should be encouraged.

2. Alter the supine head position during sleep. Techniques for accomplishing this include placing the infant to sleep with the head to one side for a week and then changing to the other, and periodically changing the orientation of the infant to outside activity (e.g., the door of the room).

3. Particular care should be taken to implement the aforementioned recommendations for infants with neurological injury or suspected developmental delay.

4. Consideration should be given to early referral of infants with plagiocephaly (flat head syndrome) when it is evident that conservative measures have been ineffective. In some cases, orthotic devices may help avoid the need for surgery.

It is critically important to be sure secondary caregivers (childcare providers, grandparents, foster parents, and babysitters) are thoroughly educated regarding these guidelines.

A recent study showed that infants do sleep more safely when a fan, providing better air circulation, is used in the room. Point the fan away from the baby so he won't be too cold.

Swaddling for Sleep

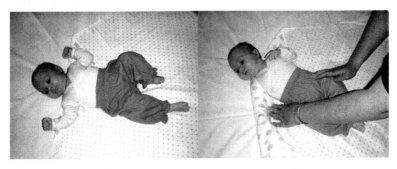

1   2

3   4

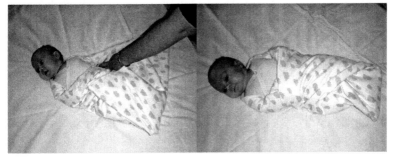

5   6

When baby is swaddled correctly, so her hands are not able to escape and find their way to her face, then she can relax. The area around a baby's face is very sensitive (like the mother's nipple) and when the blankets or the hands touch this area around her mouth, she cannot relax. Thus, with a good swaddle, baby is able to fall asleep without triggering the rooting reflex to suck and feed. The photos show my favorite swaddle technique, by wrapping the blanket over one arm first, and then bringing the corner across baby and underneath.

To swaddle baby well, place an open blanket out flat and fold one corner over, *almost* into a triangle. Place baby's neck at this folded edge. Then take the top left side of the blanket, fold it over his left arm, and hold it in place with your fingers while you wrap the left blanket corner across the body and under his bottom. Then bring the bottom corner up, just to the baby's nipple line. Give baby kicking room—don't make it too tight. For the right side, follow the same steps as the first corner: Lift the right blanket edge and bring it over the arm so the arm is in a tunnel, then bring the blanket corner across baby's body, tightly wrapping and tucking under. This immobilizes his arms. Any swaddle that keeps the arms away from the face is going to bring success. I often put another blanket, or a Swaddle Me® blanket sack by Kiddopotamus (with Velcro wings) on top of this first blanket to ensure baby does not break loose. If his hands escape from the swaddle, baby will awaken.

I know parents want to let their babies be "free" to move after so many months of cramped quarters in the womb, but baby is not ready for too much freedom just yet. A snug world is a familiar feeling to baby. Swaddling is like hugging; it settles the baby's energy.

You will know when your baby is ready to stop being swaddled when she is able to roll in both directions (front to back and back to front) and move well during playtime. This usually occurs around four to six months of age; earlier if you have given her lots of exercise. Babies have a strong startle reflex at birth and this begins to diminish as their nervous systems mature and their muscles become stronger. If you stop swaddling too soon (before three months of age) then you will have more sleepless nights. Sleep researchers have proven this. Baby can safely stay swaddled during sleep sessions in this early, immature time in her life.

When you think baby is ready to be unswaddled, try putting him down for sleep with one arm out of the swaddle first. If he copes well, then you can swaddle him with two arms free. Eventually, you will want to put baby in a sleep sack (a blanket-like fabric pouch) for his sleep sessions, which will allow him to move freely yet stay warm. Please avoid the use of loose blankets, as they can become suffocation hazards and are not recommended by the "Safe Sleep" experts. Sleep sacks made from a blanket-like fabric are a great choice when dressing baby for the cooler temperature of nighttime. I like the sleep sack that is made from a micro-fleece material manufactured by HALO®.

In a seventy-degree room, this is equivalent to putting a lightweight blanket over the baby. An added benefit is that the sleep sack prevents him from putting his feet through the open slats of the crib and getting stuck. Also, this makes it difficult for babies over eight months to stand up. Lying on the mattress and not standing, baby will fall asleep faster. I recommend the use of a sleep sack up until about age two. The sleep sack, like a blanket, can become a cue as well as an attachment object for baby; so don't be surprised if he complains when you trade the sleep sack for footed pajamas! Cutting a piece of fabric from the old sleep sack and giving it to your child can help with the transition.

Back to Sleep Time

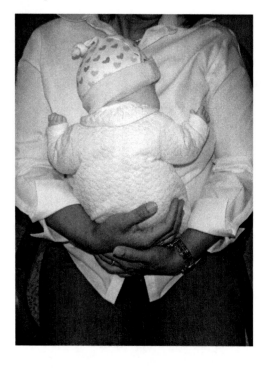

When rocking a baby, always rock her in the direction that her eyes close. Rocking from side to side is more stimulating than soothing. Thus, if rocking a baby in a rocking chair, hold her with her tummy to your tummy, her ear by your heart, facing you, but sandwiched together as shown previously. Rocking her on her back, face up in your arms isn't the best position to calm the nervous system. She may also enjoy sitting on your lap facing out, the same direction as you.

Sound and the Brain During Sleep

I have learned from the hundreds of babies I have helped that they are lulled to sleep by certain sounds. Just as the brain can be awakened by rock music, it can be quieted by soft lullaby music. Many sound machines are available to help quiet babies, but not all do the job well. Most young babies under three months of age don't seem to mind what kind of sound screen is used during their sleep sessions. The sounds of a babbling brook, ocean waves, or the wind often work but are not the ideal choice. Most inexpensive sound machines work on a loop system, repeating over and over in forty-minute cycles with a hesitation between cycles that often wakes the baby up.

The womb is a very noisy place and perhaps that is why babies seem soothed by sound. We have known for generations that saying "Shhhh … shhhh …" in their ears seems to quiet them. White noise has often been recommended to calm a fussy baby. The hair dryer, a vacuum cleaner, singing, or playing soft music all seem to help settle a baby. What I have figured out over the years is that the type of sound the brain is exposed to does seem to make a difference. The more sensitive the baby, the more important the pitch and frequency of the sound machine. The best sound machines are those that emit a sound of rushing air (similar to the wind sound produced by driving fast down a highway). This type of sound has low tones and helps elevate the alpha and delta brain waves, the ones that relax you and help you fall asleep. Using this simple device each time a baby is put to sleep becomes a sleep cue that the baby can understand. The sound screen can help block out loud home noises (like another child or dogs barking) and can help lull your baby to sleep easily, shortening crying time. When the brain detects sound in the environment on top of the sound from the machine, it is less disrupted by it and therefore not alarmed and awakened. Sound screens also work well with adult partners who have trouble sleeping (those with snoring partners)! The nice thing about using these small units (my favorite is the SleepMate® 980A by Marpac) is that you can easily pack them to take to grandma's house or on vacation. It is a great tool to block hotel noises and remind the brain it is time to rest.

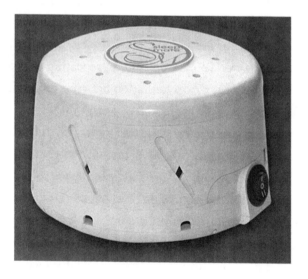

Most children seem to outgrow the need for the sound screen by about age two to three years. One day the child might say, "Please turn that machine off." This usually happens when a child is old enough to find household noises reassuring instead of alarming.

Some families use air purifiers or fans in the room. This can also provide a good noise with low tones. However, a word of caution: a fan or air cycling machine can cause the air in the room to become dry and thus cause a small baby's nose to develop dry mucus membranes. When this happens, she can get a stuffy nose and not be able to breathe well. She will then awaken crying and be unable to go back to sleep. Babies breathe through their noses and don't know how to sleep and breathe through their mouths. This can be very hard on a baby and keep her awake and restless. Some air purifiers have built-in ionizers, which can make pinging sounds when dust hits the ionizer coils. These tiny noises can also cause the baby to awaken. Sound machines that work on a loop system (such as the iPod) can also sometimes awaken a baby during the brief restart cycle.

Thus, choosing the right sound system is very important to successful sleep sessions.

Crying

Parents are uncomfortable when their children cry. It raises uneasy emotions in them. But let's face it, even adults rant, rave, and cry when bothered by something. It is a normal human expression when upset, a way of communicating and letting off steam when we don't get what we want. It doesn't mean that we should always have our way … does it? It feels good to have a voice, to let it out, to demand what you want, even if you don't always get it. What would you do if you were told you are not to get upset, not carry on loudly, and not yell about something you felt passionate about? Some people would have their world shattered if they were always told to be quiet. Babies cry to communicate. Let's face it, they yell and scream, moan and complain. So do dogs, cats, and other animals. Voices can vary depending on the creature, but we all do make noise!

Crying is the way babies reach out and say "Hey! Pay attention to me!" The challenge in listening to your baby cry is to not get too upset by this communication. Keep your cool. Observe your baby, analyze the message, and then offer him what you think he may need. This response to them is important, emotionally. Please, **do respond** to them when they cry. However, you do not need to "fix" their crying and make it stop. Sometimes we just can't; so make peace with this noise. Some babies cry more than others; we don't really know why. Perhaps it is their personality, or maybe they are simply very sensitive to the uncomfortable feelings in their bodies (gas, digestion, need to eliminate, burp, etc.). Perhaps there is a physical or emotional discomfort, or perhaps they cry in response to hunger, pain, or fatigue. Normal crying is good exercise for the lungs and also for stretching muscles of the arms, legs, and tummy. Normal crying is usually short—five to twenty minutes at a stretch—but it can happen several times a day. Sometimes, babies even cry when they are sound asleep!

When your baby cries, always ask yourself what he may need. Here are some possibilities:

Thirst, hunger, sucking, clothing change (too tight), hot or cold body temperature, gas pain, exposure to loud noises or too much light, boredom, diaper rash, pain, illness, overstimulation, or fatigue.

When baby cries after or during eating, it can be a sign that the milk (or something in the milk) is bothering her tummy. Discuss this with your baby's doctor to see if she needs a change in her diet. Parents should always attempt to figure out a baby's needs, but it isn't necessary to make the crying stop. Let your child have a voice. Sometimes they just need to get out their energy (absorbed from their noisy day). You will be able to figure out, very soon after birth, if the cry is one of discomfort or pain. Check your baby's temperature and call the doctor if you think there is a problem. Most of the time, however, the needs are simple to meet. Baby and parent must learn about each other's communication; this is a dance of approach and retreat. Make peace with the crying. It will be around for a long while.

Calming Tips for Crying

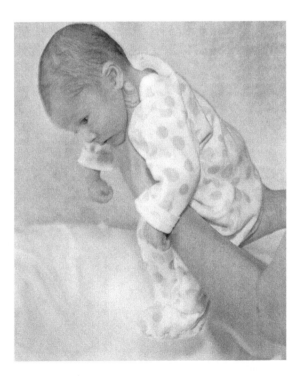

There are many different ways to hold a baby to help soothe him. My favorite and most successful way is shown in the previous photograph. I find that, more than any other hold, this works the best, unless the baby is hungry. A hungry baby will keep crying until fed. Allowing a baby's body to curve is more relaxing than keeping it straight. Bending baby into a sitting position can relax him if he is stiff or fussy. Adding a gentle up and down bounce to this position also helps. Make sure the baby's weight is forward in your hands, and his head is well supported. Since babies cannot change positions on their own, they need constant intervention by you. They like to be repositioned frequently. They need you to help them move. The more you move a baby around, the less fussy he is likely to be. Imagine being stuck in one position and unable to move!

Position baby so he is soothed and comfortable.

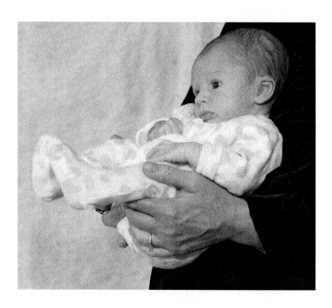

Bend and Bounce

When baby's spine is curved and stretched, she relaxes. She also is more easily able to pass gas. Motion helps settle her if she is stiff and crying.

Pacifiers

Babies love to suck! Some love it more than others. As a nurse observing this behavior for the past thirty years in the newborn nursery, I have concluded that the sucking desires of babies are genetically based. I have always wanted to do a research project on sucking and later oral behaviors to see what happens to people over time.

I postulate that the baby with a high need for sucking will grow into a person with a high oral gratification requirement. Perhaps these will be the gum chewers, the nail biters, or the candy suckers and overeaters of the world! But I can only assume, as I have never seen any research on this. My theory is that the baby who requires less sucking will probably grow up to become a thin, non-oral-oriented adult who eats to live, rather than living to eat, and prefers not to chew gum or suck on hard candy or twirl toothpicks in his or her mouth. There is nothing wrong with letting baby suck to her heart's delight in the first months.

Researchers indicate this need to suck peaks at about four months and then tapers off as babies develop more use of their hands and the ability to manipulate objects. Then they put toys and fingers into their mouths and don't require pacifiers as much. *This is the perfect time to remove the pacifier from your baby's life.* Easy to eliminate at this age, it takes only a few days and your baby will hardly miss it. If you wait until he is over one year of age, taking away the pacifier will definitely be more noticed and more emotionally traumatic.

The latest sleep research indicates that putting a young baby to sleep with a pacifier can actually lessen SIDS deaths. We think it has to do with keeping baby in the REM (lighter) sleep cycle for a prolonged time, but we don't actually know for sure. Now pediatricians are advising parents to put baby to sleep *initially* with the pacifier. *Do not reinsert it* through the night as baby continues to sleep. Parents, please realize that babies who use pacifiers do get more ear infections and may develop dental problems if used when they have teeth. Limiting or eliminating the use of the pacifier by six months of age is probably the best option.

The Importance of Tummy Time

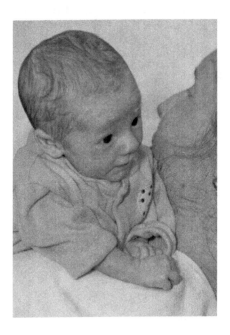

Did you know that most babies under six months rarely spend enough time on their tummies? Since the SIDS foundation has been recommending that all parents put baby down to sleep on her back, tummy time has diminished. Recently, the SIDS foundation issued a new recommendation—more tummy time! Why? Because unless a young infant can develop good strength in lifting her head and pushing up with her arms, she is at greater risk to die from suffocation or SIDS. When baby learns to roll over from back to tummy, it is important for her to have strength. If strong, she will easily be able to lift her head and breathe and move. A strong baby is a safe sleeper.

Think about how much time you are holding your baby and putting him down on his back. Most babies are deprived of the important opportunity to stretch their spines and lift their heads while positioned on their tummies. Yet the importance of tummy time has been well documented. Lack of tummy time can result in weak muscles, delays in development, and poor visual strength (switching by turns from looking into the distance to looking down at the floor strengthens eye muscles). Help your baby become stronger. Here are some suggestions for making tummy time fun and interesting:

- Get down on the floor on your tummy too!

- Encourage him, play with him, and tap tunes on the floor as if beating a drum.

- Put a mirror on the floor in front of baby's face.

- Roll up a towel and put it under your baby's chest to elevate him about six inches off the ground, a more comfortable position.

- Hold your baby so she is facing the floor, instead of facing upward.

- Lie down on the bed and put baby tummy to tummy with you for funny faces, peek-a-boo, giggles, and smiles.

- Shake a rattle or place a musical moving toy in front of baby while he stretches across your lap on his tummy.

- Place baby tummy down on a big Pilates ball and roll slightly in circles while holding him tightly.

- Place baby on her tummy on the changing table and change a diaper backward!

- Remember, *never leave baby unattended during tummy time!*

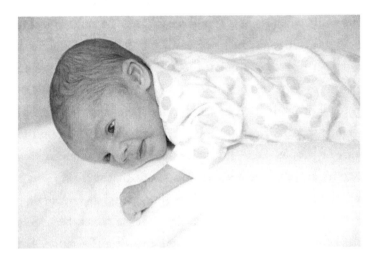

Most young infants are fairly weak and find this tummy position a bit challenging. They fuss after just a few minutes of spending time on their tummies. Be patient, for as they become stronger, they will enjoy this position more. Tummy time can be across your lap, over your shoulder, snug against your body, or draped across your arm. What you need to know about tummy time is that it is a workout to develop strength and movement and is essential for normal development. Ideally, young babies should have at least fifteen minutes or more of tummy time with each activity cycle once they are a month old. Better vision, crawling, and strength results when parents make an effort to give their baby lots of tummy time! Tummy time can be in two or three-minute increments several times a day. It is not important to have all the minutes in a row; the *total* number of minutes spent each day is what matters. A baby should be able to stay on her tummy happily for an hour by the time she is six months old.

Temperament

Who is your baby? What do you observe in his behavior? Does he startle easily when there is a loud noise? Does he smile at strangers or bury his face into you? Is he easily entertained by looking into a mirror? Is he active or quiet? Does he cling to you and not enjoy being on his own, or does he let you put him down to play on his own for short periods? Is he gaining independence over his bodily movements? Is he fussy in noisy environments and around large groups of people? Does he explore new things, or prefer to stay in Mom's arms? These are some questions that will help you gain insight into who your baby is. Personality and temperament do play a part in one's relationship with family as well as with others. "Angel" babies often adapt easily to any environment and routine. Babies with sensitive spirits have the most problems with loud stimulation. Too many people and too much noise can send them over the edge. A baby's nervous system sensors are picking up on every bit of energy in his world. A loud, bright world can easily overstimulate him. The sensitive baby can often appear to be a "colicky" or fussy baby in early infancy. You can become a more understanding and effective parent by watching for signs of your baby's temperament.

Co-Sleeping

Some parents wish to co-sleep with their baby even though it is against medical advice due to suffocation risks. If you choose to co-sleep with your little one, please make sure you are not consuming alcohol or any drugs for pain or sedation, and do not smoke. Make sure your sleeping place is free of pillows and comforters that could cover your child's face. For parents who make the decision to co-sleep with their baby, I like to recommend that they put her in a small basket or Snuggle Nest® (see photo in Chapter 1) or a cut-down plastic laundry tub while she is a young infant. That way, there are hard boundaries around the baby and she is less likely to get her face caught up in any fabric or pillows. Talk to your health professional about co-sleeping risks.

If you do choose to co-sleep, please consider relocating your baby to a crib no later than six months of age. By around six months, the baby will no longer be safe sleeping with you in bed. Babies at this age learn how to roll and crawl and can fall out of bed. If your baby is in an attached co-sleeper unit by the bed, please move your infant to a crib. If you wait any longer than this, it will be emotionally more difficult for both of you to adjust. Also, consider that adults do make noises in their sleep, and often thrash around or snore. You have no control over your actions during sleep. This can often keep your baby in a lighter sleep state. It may prevent him from sleeping well. I have had parents tell me that when they moved their baby to his own crib in his own room, everyone slept better.

Some parents choose to co-sleep with their baby even after she is six months old. Ultimately, it is a parent's choice. However, I find that if parents wait until their baby is over eight months of age to move her to a crib or into her own room, it will be more traumatic for the child. It is harder for a one-year-old to make the transition to a crib than a six-month-old. As a baby becomes more and more aware of her life and patterns, she wants consistency and routine. To safeguard your child's emotions, starting at a younger age is easier for both of you.

If you are practicing "the family bed," ask yourselves what you want for your child's future. If you want your child to sleep in his own room some day, the longer you wait (after six months) to move him there the harder it is emotionally for him to make the transition. I have known children as old as twelve still sleeping with their parents. Most children don't automatically leave the family bed at a certain age. They need to be lovingly "encouraged" out of the bed. Older children can get insomnia if moved too late in childhood to their own space, separate from their parents. It is difficult to learn to sleep alone after spending many years with others.

A new study with 29,287 infants and toddlers from many areas of the world found that parental presence at bedtime appears to have a negative effect on children's sleep. Results indicate that children who slept in a separate room got more sleep, woke less at night, had less difficulty at bedtime, fell asleep faster, and had fewer sleep problems. So, if your intention is to have your child sleeping in her own bed in her own room (at any age) then please be kind to your child's emotions and yours, and help her make the transition to her own bed no later than six to eight months of age.

Sleep Guide

Children do not react to tiredness and fatigue like adults. Lack of sleep can make very young children more active and fussy. The following guide is based on research and is recommended by sleep experts. Some children manage well with less sleep, while others need more. Look at how well your child is coping with the amount of sleep he receives to decide what is optimum for your child.

Please keep in mind that the following chart is only meant as a reference. Every child is different. Sleeping patterns differ according to how much a baby weighs at any given age, how much milk or food she is taking in, and many other variables.

Age	Hours of Needed Sleep
1 week	8 in the daytime, 8.5 at night
4 weeks	6.75 in the daytime, 8.75 at night
3 months	5 in the day, 10 at night
6 months	4 in the day, 10 at night
9 months	2.75 in the day, 11.75 at night
12 months	2.5 in the day, 11.5 at night
2 years	1.25 in the day, 11.75 at night
3 years	1 in the day, 11 at night
4 years	11.5 at night
5 years	11 at night
6 years	10.75 at night
10 years	9.75 at night

"Daniel" or A Good Schedule is Worth a Million

Sara had no rhythms or routines to her day. She felt like all her time got eaten up in caring for little baby "Daniel." It was hard just to get into the shower, not to mention fix proper meals and get some exercise. Sara called me one early morning begging me to help her get her life back on track. She found herself crabby and unfriendly and feeling depressed. Her husband worked long hours and was rarely at home. She felt isolated and lonely, as many of her friends had older children but not babies.

When I got to her home, she started to tell me how stressful it was to have no schedule, no predictability to her day. She spent most of her time holding and rocking the baby. We talked about her feelings and how she handled the simplest of errands, like the food shopping. She said Daniel was fretful every time she began to leave the house and she hesitated to subject others to her fussy baby.

We looked at how many total hours of sleep the baby got in a day, how much milk he drank (she was formula feeding), and how much awake time he had. Baby Daniel was just eight weeks old. He needed about fifteen hours of sleep a day, I told her gently. She looked at me like I was crazy. He was only sleeping about twelve hours, she told me. "How in the world am I to get him to sleep more?" she asked.

I explained the pattern of feed, diaper, play, swaddle, and sleep and she began to see the rhythm. I suggested she take the baby into the dark bedroom after he was awake for about an hour, and *before* he was acting really tired. Babies have short windows of perfect timing. It is best to catch them when they quiet down just a bit and start staring into space. That is the best time to put a baby down to sleep. I like to keep babies lightly dressed when feeding and playing; then, I wrap a nice warm blanket around them to encourage relaxation and sleep. For such a young baby, it is great to throw the blanket into the dryer for a few minutes to warm it. Once Daniel was swaddled, bounced a bit, and shhhhhed, he started to relax and began to close his eyes. I showed her how to place him in his cradle. I suggested she raise one end of the cradle to keep his head slightly elevated, as I find babies are more comfortable in this position.

Daniel fell asleep, with only a little fussing, in about five minutes. Sara was amazed.

Sometimes the smallest things you do can make a difference for some babies. In this case, I think it was the dark room and the warm blanket that worked, along with the right timing. Sara had been waiting to put her baby down for a nap until Daniel was highly fussy and falling apart emotionally. *Not good timing!*

I shared with Sara the importance of holding about a three-hour feeding window. I also told her to encourage him to take four to six ounces each feeding. I find when babies can drink consistently at least five to six ounces of milk every three hours, they are ready to start sleeping longer stretches at night. I also recommended that Sara take Daniel outside for a walk an hour each day to let him get some fresh air. I suggested that during playtime (after a feeding) she move his legs and arms for him, roll him from side to side, and offer him some tummy time until he fussed. Then give him a break for a few minutes and offer more movement. Baby might only tolerate this for five minutes at first, but eventually he will get stronger and last longer. Exercise is important even for young babies.

Sara was excited to begin her new routine and looked forward to the structure it offered. I told her that most young babies sleep about an hour with every three-hour feeding cycle. This is when she could shower, eat, e-mail, or sleep. This is your time to nurture yourself and revive. When Mommy is happy, baby is happy! As baby gets past three months of age, he will tolerate longer awake stretches, and then life will slowly get more manageable.

After about three days, Sara called me to report that she was doing well with the new plan and feeling like her arms were not always full of the baby. She was happy to report that by offering Daniel more naps, he was sleeping longer stretches. This was truly a happy ending for them both.

Chapter 4: Your One- to Three-Month-Old

Baby's Sleep Patterns the First Three Months

The first three months after birth is often referred to as the fourth trimester of pregnancy. It is appropriate to call it this because, while the baby is now outside the womb, he prefers to cling to his mother's body constantly, and stay wrapped up in a "blanket womb" most of the time, held tightly against her. The adjustment to outside life is a slowly evolving process. The baby's needs are basic: food, sleep, cleanliness, and growth, as well as your loving touch.

The first three to six months of a baby's life involve rapid growth (usually a doubling of birth weight occurs) and the beginning of muscle strengthening of her head, arms, and torso. Can you imagine what it would feel like if you, in just three months, became double your size and couldn't quite operate your limbs the way you wanted? This must feel very strange indeed. What discomforts a baby experiences in this process of growth and development is unknown, but most are somewhat fussy these first twelve weeks of life. They need constant repositioning and movement to feel content. Digesting food particles from their milk and eliminating waste products from their bodies are big transitions. They also must adapt to gravity outside the womb, since they have come from a floating, fluid environment. Please have compassion for your newborn as she begins to discover what life on planet Earth is all about and learns to adapt from a sea creature into a heavier land creature.

Surviving the fourth trimester is about creating rhythms and routines with your baby. Coping with your new life, taking care of yourself, and recovering from this huge event requires creating moments of rest and nourishment for new parents. Finding time to rest, eat, and shower is a challenge most days. As you get to know this new addition to your family, you will start to gain strength and regain yourself. As your baby strengthens and grows, so will you.

The Baby Blues or Depression?

Most women today do not realize what life changes they will encounter in having children. Birth is a transition into a less self-centered lifestyle. Therefore, there is a grieving period women sometimes go through when they realize they can no longer operate strictly according to their own needs; now their children's needs come first. It is normal to feel a little blue the first few weeks as your hormone levels are changing and you are sleep deprived. As you learn to balance baby's needs with your own and get some regular sleep periods, this tearful time should settle down and improve. Sometimes just getting a good six-hour stretch of sleep can make you feel normal again.

Don't hesitate to start offering your baby a bottle at two weeks of age (if breastfeeding). You need time to recuperate. Get your partner, family member, or friend involved and ask for help. Many couples share the evening care and take shifts. For instance, Dad will be responsible for baby from 8:00 PM to 2:00 AM, and Mom from 2:00 AM to 8:00 AM. That way each parent gets a six-hour stretch of sleep. It is usually best if the sleeping parent is in a separate room from baby so he or she can really relax and sleep without disturbance. If breastfeeding, make sure when offering your baby a bottle to choose one with a wide nipple that's recommended for breastfeeding babies. My current favorite is the Breastflow™ bottle by The First Years. Nursing moms love this system, and so do babies!

This fourth trimester can be daunting. Some women will suffer postpartum depression or the "baby blues" in adjusting to this new lifestyle. Please seek your doctor's help if you feel you are depressed or not recovering by eight to twelve weeks postpartum. Sometimes depression isn't diagnosed until even later, between six and twelve months. Sometimes the condition is due to a chemical imbalance caused by anemia or a malfunctioning thyroid.

Here are some signs of postpartum depression:

- Feeling isolated
- Wanting to sleep all the time
- Imagining harming your baby or doing strange things to him
- Not wanting to leave your home
- Crying frequently
- Being anti-social
- Having sleep disturbances
- Unintentional weight loss
- Anxiety
- Feelings of worthlessness or guilt
- Loss of sexual desire
- Lack of pleasure in activities that you once enjoyed
- Thoughts of death or suicide
- Chest pain
- Headaches
- Hyperventilating while breathing
- Feeling like you want to abandon your baby

Postpartum depression can happen anytime the first year. Please seek counseling with a health professional if you have some of the above symptoms or are concerned; sometimes there are physical causes. Some women cannot physically and mentally handle the low estrogen cycle that breastfeeding brings. Treatment with hormones may be needed to feel normal, and sometimes a woman must stop breastfeeding her baby to preserve her own health. Ask your doctor for advice.

Your life as a new parent should revolve around the feeding, awake time, and sleep sessions of your infant. If you stay in this simple pattern from the first few days home, you will gain control of life once again. Please remember to *take care of yourself first*, and then take care of your infant. You need to eat, drink, and be rested before feeding your baby. You need to think "toilet time" for yourself before changing your baby's diaper. You need to sleep when your baby sleeps. This is critical to your well-being. If you don't take care of yourself first, you may not be able to care well for your infant. A happy mother makes for a happy baby!

Support and Advice

Surround yourself with lots of support these first few months. Join a new mothers support or play group. Get out of the house and take yourself for coffee with a friend. Go for a walk or meet other new mothers at the park or in baby stores. The emotional support you gain from being around others going through the same life changes is invaluable and life sustaining. Ask your local hospital or pediatrician for resources for these groups, or search online. People will want to offer lots of advice during this early phase of parenting. Your relatives will tell you what you should be doing, and so will your friends and your doctor, and yes, even strangers. View this advice as you would the variety of books in a library. Consider it, and decide which tips you want to take down from the shelf and read more about. There are many opinions about parenting; not all of them are right for *all* babies or for *all* parents. Check in with your inner self, your intuition, and ask if this advice is right for you. Don't offend people and push them away. Just say something like, "Thank you for sharing this with me, I will consider your advice." You can avoid arguments and hurt feelings if you just listen and don't debate. You can choose whatever advice resonates with you as a parent. When asked why you aren't following certain advice a person gave you, just say, "I considered your advice, thank you. I decided it wasn't right for me and my baby." Or, "I discussed this advice with my doctor and we decided it's better to do it another way." How can someone argue with a statement like that? You will feel empowered as a parent as you create your own rules and rhythms for your family's needs.

Building Trust with Your Baby

The first three months are important for building trust between you and your baby. This process happens as a result of you responding consistently to your baby's needs. Usually, this involves feeding your baby when she shows signs of hunger (ideally before she is frantic) and talking to her with a reassuring voice when she cries. A baby quickly gets a sense that you are a consistent caretaker. It only takes a few months of repetitive positive responses to her needs for her to sense you are an important person and are dependable. This predictable caregiving creates a sense of trust between the two of you. By three or four months of age, your baby can tell which people she likes best (usually those who are consistently caring for her needs). She has begun to understand that strangers are not regularly taking care of her needs, and thus may cry when put into the arms of someone she doesn't see much or who is new to her. Deep voices may frighten her as she is programmed to respond more positively to higher pitched voices (usually those of females). This doesn't mean you should not let others hold or care for your baby—quite the opposite. I find this is an important time to teach baby that there are many adults she can trust. By frequent exposure to other loving and caring adults, she learns to trust many, not just

Mom. This will work in a positive way as she gets older and you entrust her to the care of others. It prevents whining and clingy behavior when detaching from Mother. I find it takes two or three events a week (at least an hour long) with other adults to build this attachment with others. If you want your partner to bond well with baby, don't forget to include him or her in this plan by turning over care of baby at least a few hours a week.

Ready to Sleep Longer?

Parents ask me at what age it is appropriate to let your baby fuss a bit when you put him down in the crib to sleep. There is no set answer. It should be determined both by what parents need to do for themselves, and what the baby is capable of enduring according to his development. I do believe, however, that most babies are ready to begin learning self-soothing at two to three months of age, unless born prematurely. Usually by this time, a baby is learning to use his arms and legs and can begin to bring items to his mouth to explore. This physical sign tells me he can begin to use his skills to calm his energy. Also, a baby should be over ten pounds in weight and feeding about every three hours. Baby should be consuming about five or six ounces at a time and be able to go a long stretch between feedings. If your baby is still feeding every two hours and eats small amounts each time, try pushing him to a three hour cycle and see if he will increase milk intake each feeding. Be careful if you are breastfeeding. Not all women produce abundant milk for their babies and those mothers need to continue to feed them more frequently. If this is you, wait until your baby is four months old and beginning solid foods before sleep training. Some babies are "feasters" at night and light eaters during the day. This can be due to the temperament of your baby. An active and stimulating daytime can distract baby and program him to eat lightly. A busy breastfeeding mom's milk might be less abundant during the day and baby may have learned to indulge more in the middle of the night. If you then try to cut out nighttime feedings to stretch sleep time, a baby's nutrition can suffer. In such cases, sleep training earlier than four months of age might be inappropriate unless all feedings are assessed for adequate breast milk intake.

How to Begin Sleep Training Baby

The baby should be drowsy but awake when you put her in the crib. You can start doing this from birth, but it is usually around two to three months that most parents really get serious about letting baby learn to self-soothe. Start by letting your baby fuss for five to ten minutes to put herself to sleep. A baby will not grow emotionally stronger and learn how to self-regulate if you always do something to soothe her and don't let her try to calm herself down. However, during the first three months babies still need to know you are there for them. They need to sense they can trust you and that you hear them and will take care of them. Thus, it is important to respond to a crying baby this age within a short time.

When you are trying to teach a child to walk, at first the child needs you there to hold his hands and help him, but as he practices his steps more and more, he will improve and you can encourage him to try walking without holding your hands. It is the same process for teaching self-soothing. First you respond to your baby after a short time of complaining or crying, and then you wait a bit longer. How long to let a baby fuss before you attend to his cry will depend on his age and the type of cry he makes, as well as your fortitude. If he is just complaining, not crying loudly, you might let him fuss ten to fifteen minutes and see what happens. Many babies need to "blow off steam" before they relax and go to sleep. Sleep researchers find fifteen minutes is the average time it takes a tired baby to settle and go to sleep.

If you hear the baby lessening her complaint, do not go to her. Drag your feet in responding, as she may be on the verge of calming herself and falling asleep. If your intuition senses that she is sounding anxious, then go in and touch and talk to her, saying, "Shhhh ... go to sleep, you're okay," and see if you can calm her with only your voice and touch. Use a directive voice, not one that is too soft and sweet and don't stay longer than a minute. Only pick the baby up as a last resort (after at least twenty to thirty minutes of hearing her complaints). Some parents feel better just sitting by the crib, patting the baby and saying, "Shhhh ..." and staying in the room. This is okay to try at first, but you want to position yourself so baby is not clinging to your hand. Over time, (four to five days), your goal is to get more and more physically distant from the crib. This works best with young babies under six to seven months than with older babies. Babies who can stand up will only protest longer if you are in their sight, and I don't have good success with their parents staying in the room for any length of time.

Over time, you should see that the baby is able to, on occasion, put himself to sleep. As he gains this skill, start putting the baby down awake regularly and leaving the room after a short pre-bed or pre-naptime routine. Always respond at least once if the crying continues for fifteen minutes. Acknowledge you hear his cry; tell him to go to sleep, and then leave the room again. You can repeat this if baby is still crying in another fifteen minutes. Sometimes, babies need to be picked up and consoled at the thirty-minute mark. It is fine to do this, but stay by the crib and do not walk around. Just hold the baby and say, "Shhhh ..." for one minute only, then, when he is calmer, return him to the crib and continue with the process. Try not to return again. Babies usually will fall asleep at this point.

Remember, a lot of crying loudly usually means your baby is overly tired or your perfect timing has been missed.

If baby has eaten well all day long, has had normal eliminations, and isn't ill, she should settle down within about thirty to forty minutes. I find the average time it takes for babies under nine months to settle is about twenty to forty-five minutes. It should take less and less time for her to settle the more your baby is encouraged to practice this self-soothing behavior. Most young babies learn this within a few days to a few weeks if parents are consistent with their responses. Babies often self-soothe by moving their heads back and forth, rubbing their ears, sucking their thumbs or toes, thumping their feet on the mattress, rolling side to side, or clutching a small piece of fabric. Each baby figures out what works best.

Why do you think most parents comment that their second child is calmer and easier than their first one? I believe it is because the parents are not so impulsive in responding immediately to their second baby's cry once they have had a bit of practice with their first. About 90 percent of parents remark to me that their second child is calmer and thus easier. Mother Nature doesn't deliver them that way. I believe this is because parents' experience has taught them not to pick up the second baby immediately. They know that babies do cry and they have become accustomed to listening to crying. There are other children they must attend to and they cannot possibly hold or cater to the second child as they did their first. Thus, from day one, subsequent babies self-train to be patient and learn self-soothing. This is also called self-regulation, a lifelong, critically important skill we carry with us into adulthood. Those who don't develop the ability to self-soothe early in their lives can become anxious adults. My niece (a third child) learned to self-soothe by sucking her thumb and rubbing her earlobe. As a high school student, she used to rub her earlobe to concentrate, relax, and focus during tests. These little skills learned early in life help us all life long!

Be wise parents. Those parents who both want to be involved in feeding and sleep caretaking should get involved with baby's care from the first days. Babies quickly sense that the main person who feeds them and holds them is the one to trust. If Daddy is not involved with this care, baby will take longer to develop a close relationship with him (usually it won't happen until the child is over the age of one year). So, if you want an early bonding, share care, especially the feedings. Most mothers today like this idea. They simply need to remember to praise and encourage their partners to stay involved. Don't be judgmental about your partner's ways or he or she may not stay involved with baby care.

Playtime

The most fun part of the day is when baby is awake, calm, and engaged. Playtime is learning time. The best time to teach a baby new sets of skills is during the morning and early afternoon, just after her sleep period. This is when you want to practice tummy time, rolling, sitting, standing, and walking. The key is to exercise the mind and the body. Amuse your baby with high contrast colors, new sounds, texture, and motion. Keep in mind that baby can easily get overstimulated. Exposure to artificial lighting, music, TV, loud noises, and other children can overwhelm and exhaust your little one. For young babies under three months it can happen in just fifteen minutes. Baby needs to be held and taken to a quiet place when overstimulated. If she calms easily, let her have a five- to ten-minute break and then try to reenter the play area. If she can't cope with more stimulation she may need a nap.

Be gentle with your baby after 2:00 PM, as he may have less ability to endure a lot of noise, exercise, or change in scenery. The older a baby becomes, the better he will cope with longer and longer periods of activity. The best time for any learning activity such as a gym class or music class is before 2:00 PM. Remember, prime time for baby to learn and focus is from 9:00 AM to 2:00 PM, so plan accordingly.

Getting Out of the House and Keeping Your Routine

How does one stay in a routine and still have a life outside the home? It is all about expectations. Parents need to realize it takes longer to do the same tasks than it used to now that they have a child involved. It takes more time to organize and leave the house, to get out of the car, and to get into the place you are going. Allow extra time for errands. When babies are young and need many naps each day, try to time your departure for right after a feeding. This means taking baby out and about during the prime time of the day when she can cope best. Parents need a break, too, so plan to be home by early afternoon so everyone can rest and relax. I have great compassion for today's parents. Most do too much and I see lots of exhausted parents who are sleep deprived. Adults who don't sleep six to eight hours a day are not healthy parents. Make your sleep needs a priority as well as your child's.

You will have one to two hours to do what you need to do between feedings. If your baby falls asleep in the car seat on the ride home, just leave him in the car and read a book while you wait for him to awaken. If he falls asleep in the stroller on a walk, again, leave him in the stroller until he finishes the nap. After a baby is past three months old, it is important to try to ***never move him during his sleep state***. This will cause emotional anxiety over time, and a more distrustful and wakeful baby. My advice is let baby sleep wherever he falls asleep until he awakens. You may awaken him and be assured he's had a decent amount of sleep after he has slept at least forty-five minutes. Yes, it is a short nap, but better than none. Extra naps may be needed when the day naps are short. Remember, most children under age one need three to four total hours of daytime sleep.

If a baby is under two months of age, she will be unaware of being moved in her sleep, so it probably wouldn't affect a really young baby adversely. But, after two to three months of age, be respectful and let baby sleep where she is for the entire sleep session. In moving a baby, parents often wake the baby and then are unable to get her back to sleep, so take care to keep the environment the same as where she fell asleep. No adult wants to be moved during sleep, so why treat a baby that way? If baby falls asleep in your arms, you should hold her the entire sleep time. Again, this is respectful care. At two to three months of age, it is time for you to correct any poor patterns and cues you have developed. What are they, you ask? Things like rocking baby, holding her until sleep, playing music to fall asleep, using a stroller or swing to nap your baby, moving a baby after she is asleep, bouncing baby to sleep, and even using a pacifier to help her fall asleep (unless she can use it only to fall asleep and doesn't need it reinserted all night long).

Consistency is Key

The way a baby learns new things is by repetition and consistency, by using what I call "black and white" behavior. He doesn't perceive "gray" areas. In other words, if you want your baby to fall asleep in his crib, then always put him in his crib for naps and night sleep. If he is in other places like a stroller or a swing when he falls asleep, he will not necessarily associate the crib with sleep. This is not to say that your baby can never nap some place other than the crib. It just means that while you are helping him form new habits, you must think about places, tools, and techniques. So, for a period of time, say, two to four weeks, please try to be consistent so baby can learn.

Yes, it is a sacrifice at first. You must be home more. But it is worth it. Your baby will learn flexibility as he becomes older. The first six months are a very formative time. It is best to be consistent in your teaching. Create rituals around sleep time so baby learns what is coming. Link behaviors such as feeding and diaper changing so baby trusts what you are doing with him and when. The world would be a more stressful place if we didn't have predictability to our lives. I notice a calmer baby when his environment and routines are predictable. If he has no understanding of what will happen next, he will have some stress and be more irritable. Even if your baby is in daycare, try to get him a consistent caregiver so he learns to establish trusting bonds with caring adults.

The Fussy Baby, Special Needs

The fussy or out of sorts baby is usually a very sensitive soul. She feels the world more intensely than others. It is as if a layer of protection has been removed from her nerves. She hears things more loudly and feels things more strongly. Wouldn't it be wonderful if we could figure out this baby's needs right from day one? Usually, parents sense their baby is one who wants to be held and swaddled from the first weeks. She cries more than other babies. She may be referred to as a "colicky" baby. Some babies have gastrointestinal reflux or other health conditions. By definition, a fussy baby is one who cries more than two or three hours a day. I find these children need lots of hands-on attention. I sense they feel vulnerable in our very loud and bright world. It is important to have some help so you don't become emotionally depleted. Whether bouncing, feeding, carrying baby next to your body, or just sitting and holding this infant, it is a very time-consuming job. It will be a challenge just to get a shower and a meal. Parents, please hear this: you are not a bad parent if you need to put the baby down for fifteen minutes in a safe place and take a break. If you are at the end of your rope, put the baby in the crib and take fifteen minutes to breathe in some air and see the sun. Recuperate. Then you will be a better parent when you return to attend to your baby. Sometimes I have found that a fussy baby is more bothered by tags and tightness in clothing, the texture of rough fabric, bright sun, wearing hats, etc., so be sure to check if anything baby is wearing is tight or bothersome. Give her plenty of wiggle room. Make sure there are no tight elastic bands, tight socks on the feet, or tags poking out. I also find that if clothes are too tight fitting and baby can't stretch, it is uncomfortable for her and then she cries more. Try this experiment: take all her clothes off and see if she quiets down. If she does, gradually add one item back at a time and see what happens. Often, you can figure out the bugaboo just by slowly reapplying clothes!

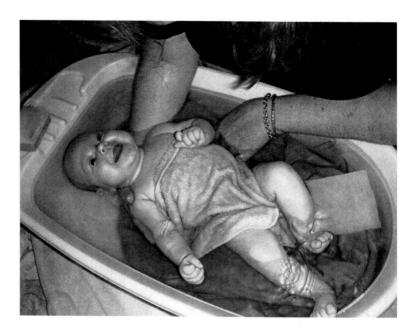

Another thing that sometimes settles babies is to give them a warm bath. Be sure there is plenty of warm water (almost up to the neck) so baby can float around, relax, and enjoy the bath. Cover the chest with a wet washcloth to keep baby warm. Play with him gently and let him relax. After your floating session, you can wash baby quickly and take him out. Dry him, and see if he will tolerate a little massage with a lavender lotion (it will help quiet the spirit). But don't pursue any massage strokes that make your baby fussy. Ask for his permission to massage him. Start with his legs and feet and gradually work up. Be gentle and go slowly. Stop when your baby indicates he doesn't want any more. You can learn baby massage at many parenting centers, or even online.

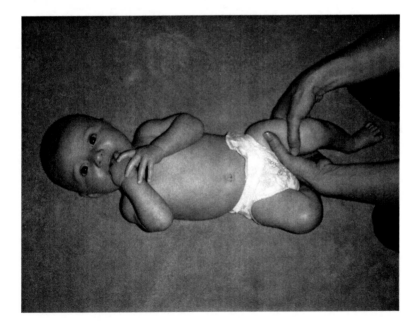

Most fussy babies (and sensitive babies) need more sleep. Make sure to offer your young infant a nap after at least every ninety minutes she is awake. Think this way: ninety minutes awake, ninety minutes asleep, and then offer another feeding. This is your three-hour cycle. You may be surprised; she might just cry less when she is a well-rested infant.

Recently, I read about a study done in Sweden in which the researchers looked at different groups of fussy babies who had no apparent reason for their fretful behavior. In this study, they found that giving infants probiotic drops with their food daily helped reduce crying by more than half. Discuss this option with your baby's doctor. In the study, BioGaia® probiotic drops worked better than any other remedy such as simethicone drops. Probiotics can rebalance the intestinal flora of an infant and thus cut down on gas and tummy pain. I say it's worth a try!

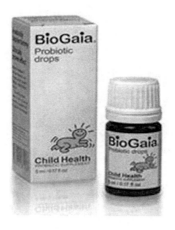

Baby Sleep Schedule

Example of a Day/Night Rhythm

Birth to Three Months

6:00 AM   Baby awakens. You offer milk shortly after he wakes up.

6:30 AM   Feeding finished. Change diaper.

7:00 AM   Playtime—don't forget to offer lots of tummy time!

7:30 to 8:00 AM   Baby is tired and needs a nap. Put baby in the crib and let her fuss to sleep. Go in after fifteen to twenty minutes only if baby is crying loudly. Say firmly, "Shhhh ... go to sleep," and leave the room. Return and repeat after another fifteen to twenty minutes if baby is still crying loudly. Drag your feet in returning if baby is crying "off and on" and not loudly. It may take some time, but eventually, as the baby learns to fall asleep, this time will lessen to about five to ten minutes of fussy behavior. It is okay to start with five minutes of crying (not fifteen minutes of crying) for babies under four months old. Just keep practicing until it becomes longer periods.

9:00 to 10:00 AM   Baby awakens. Offer milk shortly thereafter. Change diaper and have playtime when feeding is finished. After about one-and-a-half to two hours of awake time, offer another nap. This feed, diaper, play, sleep pattern will continue until bedtime.

6:00 to 9:00 PM   Bedtime. Be sure to offer a sleep routine such as feeding, bathing, dressing for bed, rocking, and cuddling, and then into the crib *awake.* Turn lights out, and let baby fuss until she falls asleep. This can take fifteen to sixty minutes at first but should shorten with time. About two hours after baby falls asleep, offer a "dream" feeding.

9:00 to 11:00 PM   Dream feed if baby is under fourteen pounds. It is important that you *do not* wait until baby cries and then go in to feed. Go into baby's room when he is still asleep and gently wake and feed. You need to be the boss of when the feeding will happen, not him. You can even stand at the crib edge and just offer a bottle while baby stays in the crib and is drowsy. *Do not* prop the bottle. Just lift the baby's head up and put the nipple in his mouth. Try to get the baby to eat as much as possible. Usually I find babies won't take more than a few ounces. This is a sign they are really getting ready to begin sleeping six to eight hour stretches or longer. If your baby only takes two ounces at this feeding time, try eliminating the dream feeding the next night. If baby awakens from the time of the last feeding until morning (6:00 AM), just say, "Shhhh …" and tell him to go back to sleep. Remember to wait fifteen minutes until you go in if he awakens crying. *Only go into the room if he is loudly crying.* Don't go into the room if the baby is crying in an "on and off" pattern, as this is a sign he is trying to let go and go to sleep by himself. Your presence will interrupt his process.

For twins or multiples, it is sometimes easier to separate babies for a few weeks until they learn the art of falling asleep. Then you can move them back into the same room as the pattern is better established.

Remember, babies often react to fatigue by being more active (and fussy). If this happens, you've missed your perfect window of timing and baby may need to cry longer to tire herself again. Too early to bed is better than too late to bed.

"Victoria" or A Baby with Severe Reflux

I was excited to meet baby "Victoria." I love challenges, and she posed several. Her mother, whom I will call "Christine," was a first-time mom and eager to help her baby get more sleep. She had to hold Victoria upright most of the time so she wouldn't spit up. Whenever the baby was put in her crib, she tended to cry and get tense and eventually scream in apparent pain. The only way mom could deal with this baby was by holding her upright, tummy to tummy. After three months, she was exhausted.

When I met baby Victoria, she was in her swing and gave me a big smile. She seemed happy in this moment, but Christine told me it was because her stomach wasn't full. She was due for a feeding in about thirty minutes.

We discussed reflux and the challenges it presented. I shared with Mom how important it was to put the baby down for sleep when her stomach was neither empty nor full. A baby with reflux has a weak stomach sphincter and cannot contain her food well if there is pressure against this muscle. Being put flat creates such pressure and makes acid escape into the esophagus, causing pain. In adults with reflux, it is recommended they not consume food for four hours prior to bedtime to avoid pain. In babies I find it is best to stop feeding at least thirty minutes prior to sleep.

While Christine had some good rhythms already established, she was feeding her baby to sleep and then putting her down. I suggested this likely created the problem.

I sat with baby Victoria and Mom through the next feeding. Mom explained that she had tried many different formulas and it seemed most of them bothered her baby in some way. Some gave her baby a lot of gas, some she wouldn't drink much of and then would cry, and one even made blood appear in the stool. I suggested she try a hypoallergenic formula. In my experience, milk protein or formulas containing lactose can pose more problems for baby. Christine had tried to breastfeed, but the baby wouldn't latch well and would fuss and pull off. Eventually, out of desperation to get her baby to eat, she tried formula in a bottle.

Christine and her pediatrician had recently discussed switching to the hypoallergenic formula, so with my encouragement, she said she would give it a try. After baby Victoria finished her feeding of four ounces of formula, she started to fall asleep. We tickled her feet, rubbed her back, and moved her around until she opened her eyes and stayed awake. I discussed the importance of activity time *after* a feeding. I told her that baby had just gotten fuel, and now needed to be active and utilize some of this fuel before rest time. The baby gladly played with us and was in a good mood. We kept her upright in our laps. After about an hour, she began to fuss a bit, and since she had not slept in almost two hours, I suggested we put her down for a nap.

I showed Mom how to swaddle so the blankets were not in her face, and we turned on the sound machine, closed the drapes, and whispered gently that it was time to sleep. Mom rocked her a few minutes and said, "Shhhhh ... go to sleep."

She put Victoria down in the crib on a foam cushion designed for babies with reflux. Victoria fussed harder as we walked away from her. We began to watch the clock. After about five minutes, she began to cry less. There were pauses in her crying. I pointed out to Mom that this was a good sign that Victoria was starting to self-settle. But, a few minutes later, she ramped up her cry again, so we approached her and patted her and again and gave her a pacifier and said, "Shhhh ... go to sleep." We walked away again and gave her some time. After about three more minutes of loud crying, she started to settle and go to sleep.

Over the course of the next few days, Christine practiced the new pattern of feeding, playing, and then sleep. She started the hypoallergenic formula and noticed the baby would drink more each feeding. She also noticed that the sleep cycles started to lengthen and instead of just a twenty-minute nap, Victoria was able to sleep an hour or more each nap. Her nighttime sleep also lengthened. She was getting a six-hour sleep stretch! Before our plan began, she was lucky to get just two hours of sleep before another feeding.

I am happy to report that this mother and baby did well. While it took a few more months for Victoria's reflux to improve,

Christine had learned how to deal with this medical problem so her baby was growing well, sleeping well, and no longer in any discomfort.

I notice babies with reflux are highly sensitive. They do not tolerate imbalances in their environment. They complain more when too many people stimulate them, too much noise exists, or feedings are irregular. Learning your baby's own needs isn't always easy, but with professional help, things can rapidly improve. Always seek the advice of a nurse or doctor if you are struggling with baby reflux problems such as this.

Chapter 5: Your Three- to Six-Month-Old

Creating a Good Day/Night Rhythm and a Self-Soothing Baby

Generally, no matter what age the child, the steps to raising a good sleeper are the same. Teaching the child how to put himself to sleep is the key. Your part is to let go and let him. As I described in brief earlier, a child can put himself to sleep by thumping a foot against the mattress, rolling his head back and forth, humming, stroking the edge of a satin blanket, sucking a thumb, curling up into a favorite position, rocking, or other self-soothing activities. How children learn to self-soothe often follows them into adulthood. *This is an important skill to develop that will serve your child for the rest of his life.* Anxiety is often a result of a child's inability to learn self-soothing. So, teaching a baby about sleep in the first year of life is a valuable gift you can give to your child. Like riding a bike or learning to drive, it is not a skill easily learned in a short time. One has to grasp it through practice, experience, and struggle. It is similar to learning the art of balance. No one can teach you balance; you have to discover how it works on your own. I encourage you to begin helping your child learn this skill early in the first year of life.

Is your baby ready to sleep six or more hours a night? Is she taking five to six ounces of breast milk or formula at each feeding and able to go three hours between feedings? When a baby is physically big enough and is taking larger and larger amounts of milk each feeding, she is ready to be sleep trained. Some babies achieve this goal at two months of age, but most achieve it by three to four months. Short nighttime sleep stretches are related to small frequent feedings (more than eleven in twenty-four hours). Thus, try to encourage baby to feed at about three-hour intervals. Some babies can't go three hours from feeding to feeding. This can be a sign that sleep training is not yet appropriate. You may need to wait until solid foods are included in your baby's diet.

How to Build a Framework for Good Sleep Habits

I like to recommend that you begin with bedtime. First, about an hour beforehand, tell your child that things will be different from now on. Explain the new rules. Tell him what you want from him and what you are going to do (or not do) when he wakes up in the middle of the night. When you hear your child cry, don't rush to him in the first minute you hear him. Sleep researchers say that it takes on average, ten to fifteen minutes for a child to relax and quiet his body, and then fall asleep. *Never* ignore a child crying out to you; this is emotional abandonment that can have lasting effects. I do not recommend this! *Always* respond and let your child know you hear him. But, this doesn't mean you have to go to him immediately or give him what he is calling out for—usually you, his human teddy bear. Allow your child ten to fifteen minutes by himself to try to settle on his own. Listen to the type of cry he makes. Usually, there are a few minutes of silence, then five to ten minutes of angry and loud crying. In his own language he is saying, "I don't want to go to bed, I want to stay up and be part of the party. Come and get me. How could you make me go to bed now?" Sound familiar? Do you remember being a child, begging your parent to let you stay up longer? Most children resist detaching from their parents at bedtime, so be assured that this behavior is very normal.

Letting baby voice her feelings is healthy. Just because she wants to stay up, doesn't mean a parent should let her. Trust your decision. If you know she is tired, then give her a chance to put herself to sleep. To go back into your child's room and pick her up when you see clearly that she is tired is not good parenting. Be patient. Let the baby complain. Some need to blow off steam from their stimulating day. Crying can be releasing. Shortly, you will hear more inconsistent crying, what I call "off and on crying." This is a glimpse at the child trying to let go and fall asleep. If she succeeds, she will go into a deep slumber. If she doesn't succeed, she will start with the loud crying again. At this point, if it has been ten to fifteen minutes, then it is time to communicate to her that you hear her. If this happens, send in the strongest, most authoritative parent (usually Dad) and say something like, "Shhhh ... go to sleep, baby ... quiet now, you are fine." Make it brief and then leave the room. This can also be done at the crib side (you can even sit on a nearby chair with your back to the child), or when the child is older, from the doorway. Give her another opportunity to fall asleep by again retreating into another room. Usually the next five minutes will be loud crying. Another exclamation from the baby, "How could you leave me here? I am mad at you!" Shortly, you will hear another attempt at quieting down. Usually, with a baby under six months of age, sleep will follow very shortly. On average, in my experience, it takes twenty to forty-five minutes for babies to let go and fall asleep when you first begin this new method.

Whew. You did it! Now your child is on the path to better sleep. Older or strong-willed children may continue alternating between intense crying and off and on crying for an hour or more. Eventually they do give up and go to sleep. I often find this is a longer process when children have been exposed to a lot of stimulation or are overly tired. With a child who is well rested, it should not take more than an hour for him to let go and fall asleep.

Sleep-deprived children have more adrenaline and cortisol (wake up hormones) in their systems and it is harder for them to fall asleep. Strange as it seems, the more a child is in a quiet environment and the more naps she takes, the better sleep she gets at night and the easier it is for her to fall asleep again and again day and night. During sleep, your body produces sleep hormones that make you groggy. The more sleep, the more your hormone levels stay elevated, thus the easier it is to go back to sleep. I think of this process of letting baby cry when put down as "letting go of energy." When you are energized, it is hard to stop and be quiet. Activity is what will exhaust you and bring you to the place of sleep. For a young child, this activity often happens in the crib with crying, tossing, jumping, or rolling, until at last, sleep comes. Sweet bliss. I find that most of the time, the parent is the anxious one and the difficult one to train, not the child.

Another Option

It is very hard for a parent to listen to his or her child crying. I realize how tough this can be. If it makes you feel better, you can offer your physical presence to your child and sit next to the crib or bed until he eventually lets go and falls asleep. However, if you choose this path, be aware that you, too, are an object that will require weaning. You are like the human teddy bear, easy to cling to and hard to give up. Be prepared for a longer training period, usually three or four weeks. Many parents tell me they can't emotionally handle sitting by the crib, listening to their child cry, and doing nothing to console him. Don't try this method if this is you. You must be a very strong-willed person to follow this plan. It helps to make it a short project. Try each day to gradually move the chair farther away from the child's bed until you are out the door. If you carry on with the plan for each sleeping session, be it nap or bedtime, I promise results over time. You will see, as each day passes, it will get easier. *But you must be consistent.* Learning happens with practice and consistent responses. If you give in and take the child out of his bed, and then rock, feed, or take him to your bed, *you will undo all your hard work.* It will be worse on your child the second time around, and especially difficult for you. If you stick to the plan, in a short time there will be less crying, more sleep, a happier child, and happier parents. These are the results to expect after three or four days (longer for those who choose to remain in the room). Most parents report that after twenty-four hours, they see improvement in the time it takes for their child to fall asleep. This indicates that the child is learning to self-soothe. You're making progress!

Children look to you for guidance. They like to know where the boundaries are. You create the walls. The process of sleep training reminds me very much of my own driving lessons. At first everyone is nervous; we make some mistakes, but eventually we all feel less fearful because we know there are rules of the road, speed limits, and signs guiding us. We gain confidence the longer we continue to drive. Without these guidelines, driving is chaos and anxiety-ridden. Think about it. This is how your children feel when they don't know the rules of the road. Help them feel safe and know what life is about. We do need to have a sense of rhythm to our day (and night). We are all creatures of habit. Your job as a parent is to help your children advance down the path, teaching them skills that will enable them to become independent, self-sustaining human beings.

Sleep Cycles

According to the research on sleep in children, an average sleep cycle lasts about sixty to ninety minutes. For babies, the first thirty to forty minutes of each cycle is deep sleep and the second thirty to forty minutes is REM, or active sleep. As we age, the REM portion of the cycle shortens. In old age, REM sleep only lasts about ten minutes. Research shows that REM sleep is important because it is then that we incorporate new tasks, language, and other facts into our brains for long-term storage. Learning can be diminished if one does not have enough REM sleep. We don't need a lot of REM sleep when we are older because we are not learning as much. Children who do not get enough sleep don't learn as easily. I think of REM, or active sleep, as the most important part of the sleep cycle. I call it "computer-downloading" time for the brain. This precious time is when all new tasks and information are organized into the brain's inner structure for future retrieval. In infants, it is half of their sleep cycle, and it is very important. Babies often wake when making the transition from the deep sleep cycle into the active sleep cycle. You can tell when your baby is in this lighter sleep phase because you see eye movements, sucking, and physical activity.

If you have a sensitive baby who hears your voice or the phone ringing or feels cold, it is likely that she will awaken during this period of sleep since it is a light sleep state. Many babies wake after a thirty-minute nap because they are pulled out of this transition time by noise, light, cold, or other discomforts. You hear the baby cry and you think she is waking up and you may rush in to get her up. Yes, babies do cry in their sleep. If the baby's eyes are closed, she is probably still sleeping. Don't hurry in and pick her up quickly, as this won't allow her to naturally awaken slowly. If we don't complete our REM sleep cycle, we awaken groggy and a little out of sorts. We have all experienced this "daze" when our alarm clocks awaken us in the middle of a dream. Babies wake themselves up gradually, but often if given ten minutes, they will fall back to sleep and continue the very important REM phase of sleep. Sleep experts feel that if a baby does not sleep for at least an hour, she does not fully rest. I have known babies who only seem to need a forty-five minute nap, but I think this is minimum. Too short a nap can lead to fussy and inattentive babies. If your baby is sensitive, try having a sound machine play near the crib. It can help the brain tune out the environmental noises in the background. I find the best sound machine is the SleepMate® 980 by Marpac (available online).

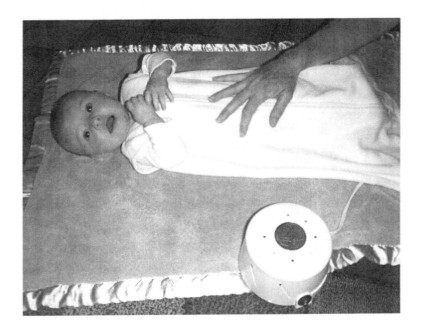

Playing music during sleep is not a good idea, as it is filled with too many varying tones and the ear and brain cannot fully relax and sleep deeply. It can be good for pre-bedtime routines, but not as a sleep aid. Don't worry about your child getting too attached to this sound machine noise. I find most children don't want it on anymore when they become toddlers and are comforted by the noises of the house. When language develops and they have learned the kinds of noises people make, house sounds become reassuring instead of alarming. They often ask you to turn off the machine at about two to three years of age. If your baby wakes up happy and smiling, it is usually a good sign he has had enough sleep and completed his REM cycle before awakening. If he wakes up crying and fussy, he probably needs more sleep. Use your intuition and over time you will learn what his needs are. The sleep guide at the end of Chapter 3 shows hours of sleep needed according to age. I hope this helps you figure out if your child is getting enough sleep.

Physical Activity

We in the health professions have noticed that babies have fallen behind in their physical development since the SIDS Foundation began recommending that they be put down to sleep only on their backs. Recently, the Foundation issued a new recommendation—that babies should spend more of their waking time on their tummies. Why? Because a young infant needs to develop good strength in lifting her head and pushing up with her arms.

A baby is at greater risk of dying from suffocation or SIDS if he is without good strength and control of his head, upper body, and torso. When baby learns to roll over from back to tummy, it is important for him to have strength. If strong, he will easily be able to lift his head and breathe and move. A strong baby is a safe sleeper. Work with your baby from three to six months of age to teach him how to roll in both directions. Be your baby's coach. He may get frustrated, so work in short ten to fifteen minute sessions, two or three times a day. As the baby builds strength, he will easily achieve developmental milestones appropriate for his age. If baby isn't rolling in both directions and sitting well by nine months, please ask your physician for a referral to a pediatric physical therapist, neurologist, or other health professional for an assessment.

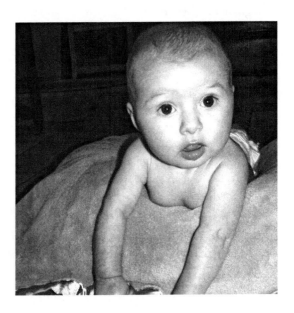

Think about how much time you are holding your baby, putting your baby in the swing or car seat, and putting him down on his back. Most babies are deprived of the important (and frequent) time to stretch their spines and lift their heads while positioned in seated positions. Yet the importance of tummy time has been well documented. Delays in development and poor visual strength can result from weak muscles.

Please help your baby become stronger by encouraging her to spend time on her tummy when she is awake. By the time she is six months old, she should be happily willing to spend an hour on her tummy. In Chapter 3, The Importance of Tummy Time, you will find an extensive list of suggestions for the many ways you can make the time interesting and enjoyable for both you and your baby as she builds her strength.

Teething

Babies can begin teething around four to six months of age or even later. Some babies show no distress or discomfort and others are irritable and in pain, chewing on their fingers and rubbing their gums. When teething, a baby can drool, have a runny nose, swollen gums, and hyper-acidity of the stomach. It can be helpful to use a wet piece of gauze wrapped around your finger to massage the gums. This oral activity can decrease gum pain. Use it daily starting when your baby is around three months of age; clean the gums and tongue by rubbing gently. This also introduces the idea of putting something into the mouth for cleaning and will help ready your infant for later tooth hygiene.

Irritable, teething babies need relief. There are several options. I like to recommend that you begin with a homeopathic remedy such as "Teething Tablets" by Hylands™ or a single homeopathic remedy called "Camomilla." You can find these at your local health food store or pharmacy. If neither helps, try giving Infant Tylenol® drops (check with your doctor or pharmacist for the correct dosage). Using a gel that numbs pain directly on the gums may also offer temporary relief. If your baby spits up excessive amounts or smells a bit acidy, discuss with your doctor about using an anti-gas product or children's probiotic. Since saliva produces digestive enzymes each time baby puts toys or hands in his mouth, this excess oral stimulation and exposure to bacteria can upset the tummy. Loose stools and acid stomach can result.

Remember to wash your baby's hands and toys after every diaper change, and clean toys frequently.

Infants are not all distressed by teething, but for those who are, it can be difficult to sleep train during teething times. If you are already in the process when you notice some of these teething symptoms, don't stop unless your baby is uncomfortable. Sometimes teething or illness can be a setback. Always consider your baby's emotional and health needs first. Trust your instincts. Nights with a sick baby can be unpleasant. You may need to just hold baby all night and forget about your sleep framework for a time. There is no better way. This is just a temporary setback. You can restart again when baby is well.

Introducing Solid Foods

Usually, sometime between four and six months, pediatricians recommend that you begin introducing solid foods to baby. The first food may be rice cereal, vegetables, or fruit. Many choices exist, so it is best to discuss how to begin with your baby's doctor. After your baby has tolerated one meal a day well for a few weeks, you can add more and more food choices and increase the number of meals offered daily. This introduction of solid foods initiates the weaning off formula or breast milk. The process of gradual milk reduction will result in less and less milk being consumed while adding more and more solid foods. By the time baby is one, milk intake is usually reduced to about half the amount taken earlier.

Did you know that twelve to sixteen ounces is usually the recommended daily quantity of milk intake for a one-year-old? Offer three to four servings of about three to four ounces in a sippy cup or bottle. This reduction in milk intake is suggested for a few reasons. Your child needs increasing amounts of protein, iron, and fat, as well as vitamins and minerals. These are important for brain and body growth. If your baby has too much milk, the calcium can inhibit iron absorption and cause anemia. And too much milk, in conjunction with more nutrients from solid foods, can also lead to obese infants and toddlers (and a possible risk of developing diabetes when older). If a baby doesn't get the nutrients she needs, she will not grow well and be healthy. I often come across infants in my practice who are drinking way too much milk and not receiving enough solid foods. This can affect their sleep patterns as well as their growth and satiation. If you need help figuring out how much to feed your baby and when, please seek professional advice from a pediatric dietician or nutritionist. Again, this is the time you should be forming good feeding habits and creating well-rounded eating behaviors. Nobody wants a picky eater. Good nutrition is just as important as good sleep habits.

Post-term babies (those born after forty weeks gestation) and big babies, whose bodies mature earlier than others, are often ready for solid foods sooner. Don't stress too much during this phase if baby isn't taking much each meal. A baby usually begins eating well after nine months of age. At that point, you can begin to include foods from your plate. Variety becomes more important, and I find most babies prefer our food to commercial baby foods.

By nine months, a baby should be eating about a quarter to half a cup of food, three times a day. Provide milk four times between meals (three to four ounces each serving). If you want to encourage baby to eat solid food, try offering it to him when he wakes from a good sleep and is in a happy mood. Hold the milk until about an hour after the solids. You don't want baby too hungry or he won't be able to focus on eating. Experiment with the timing until you understand his needs. Make sure to offer him a few sips of water from a cup during mealtime. Babies learn how to swallow their food by sucking. So, at first, you will notice baby needs to suck on his hand in order to swallow the food. If your baby is on the young side (four to six months) when you introduce solid food, it may be necessary to offer a bit of food on the end of your fingertip first. Then, let him suck it off. Make sure the food is very moist at first. You should be able to pour it off your finger. If it sticks to your finger and doesn't dribble down, it is too thick.

Food temperature is important as well. Make sure baby's food is barely warm or at room temperature. Baby might reject the food if it is too cold or too hot. Feeding her can be fun but it is also messy. A baby should be able to sit well and reach out to grab a spoon from your hand when you start solid food feedings. These are developmental signs that tell us your baby is ready to eat. Getting teeth is Mother Nature's way of reminding parents that baby needs to eat solid food, however, not all babies have teeth before feeding begins. Follow your doctor's advice. As a precaution, it is a good idea to learn infant CPR and choke-saving skills before beginning this adventure.

There are products on the market that make feeding safer. Small net bags that screw on to a small handle allow infants to learn about feeding easily. The baby sucks on the net bag and strains foods into his mouth. Cold or frozen fruit is great to insert into these devices. It can be a good teething remedy and it's a fun toy! Designs 2-U, Inc. makes one called the Baby Safe Feeder™, pictured below.

Baby Sleep Schedule

Example of Day/Night Rhythm

<u>Three to Six Months</u>

<u>6:00 AM</u> Baby awakens. You offer milk shortly thereafter.

<u>6:30 AM</u> Finished with feeding. Change diaper.

<u>7:00 AM</u> Playtime—don't forget to offer lots of tummy time!

<u>7:30 to 8:00 AM</u> Baby is tired and needs a nap. If she is not yet self-soothing, keep working on it as follows: Put her in the crib and let her fuss to sleep. Go in after fifteen to twenty minutes if baby is crying loudly. Say, "Shhhh ... go to sleep," (firmly) and leave the room. Return and repeat after another fifteen to twenty minutes if baby is still crying loudly. Drag your feet in returning if baby is crying "off and on" and not loudly. It may take some time, but eventually, as the baby learns to fall asleep, this time will lessen to about five to ten minutes of fussy behavior. It is okay to start with five minutes of crying and not fifteen minutes of crying for babies under four months old. Just keep practicing until it becomes longer periods.

9:00 to 10:00 AM   Baby awakens. Offer milk shortly thereafter. Change diaper and have playtime when feeding is finished. Baby should be happy for at least two hours. Offer a feeding at about the two-hour mark since last feeding (in anticipation of nap coming up). Keep baby awake for at least fifteen minutes after this feeding, and if he is tired, offer a mid-day nap sometime around 1 to 3:00 PM. Remember, baby should sleep about one to two hours and no more than four hours total in the daytime at this age. Sleeping too much in the day can lessen the need for sleep at night. But too little sleep can shorten nighttime sleep stretches due to lack of sleep hormones building in the body. For most babies in this age group, three to four hours of daytime sleep is ideal. But if baby sleeps less than ten hours a night, more naps are needed.

5:00 to 9:00 PM   Bedtime. Maintain the sleep routine such as feeding, bathing, dressing for bed, rocking and cuddling, and then into the crib *awake*. Turn lights out, and let baby fuss until she falls asleep. This can take fifteen to sixty minutes at first, but should shorten with time. About two hours after baby falls asleep, offer a dream feeding.

9:00 to 11:00 PM   Dream feed if baby is under fourteen pounds. It is important you ***do not*** let baby cry and then go in to feed. Go into baby's room when he is still asleep and gently wake and feed. You need to be the boss of when the feeding will happen, not him. You can even stand at the crib edge and just offer a bottle while baby stays in the crib and is drowsy. *Do not prop the bottle.* Just lift the baby's head up and put the nipple in the mouth. Try to get the baby to eat as much as possible. Usually I find babies won't take more than a few ounces. This is a sign they are really getting ready to sleep for a six to eight hour stretch or longer. If your baby only takes two ounces at this feeding time, try eliminating the dream feeding the next night. From the time of the last feeding until morning (6:00 AM) if baby awakens, just say, "Shhhh …" and tell him to go back to sleep. Remember to wait fifteen minutes until you go in if he awakens crying. *Only go into the room if he is loudly crying.* Don't go into the room if the baby is crying in an "on and off" pattern, as this is a sign he is trying to let go and go to sleep himself. Your presence will interrupt his process of going to sleep.

Remember, babies often react to fatigue by being more active (and fussy). If this happens, you've missed your perfect window of timing and baby may need to cry longer to tire herself again. Too early to bed is better than too late to bed.

"William" or Moving the Baby Out of Your Bed

A mother from Florida called me to discuss how she might get her baby, "William," back into the crib after spending several months sleeping together. Daddy had been called to fight the war in Iraq, and he would soon be returning. She wanted the bed to be a baby-free zone.

After spending months sleeping with your baby, there usually is a time when parents realize that enough is enough. The best time to consider moving baby out of your bed is *before* he is a year old. It becomes quite difficult, emotionally, for a baby to have the rules change if he has spent many months sharing a bed with the parents. My biggest concern for babies who have been co-sleeping is from a safety standpoint. Most parents don't think about the tragic accidents that can happen from a baby falling out of his parent's bed. The truth is, many deaths and accidents related to falls happen daily. A baby can also become a victim when he reaches the crawling stage, so please take heed.

A parent's job is to protect his or her young. When you decide your baby is ready to move to the crib (or should I say, when you are ready), then talk to him about this new sleeping arrangement. Many parents think that it is easier to keep a crib in their room and move the baby to another room in stages. I do not think this matters unless the baby is very young (under six months). I have found that most parents find it easier on their relationship and their child if the child has his own room and his own sleeping space. A family that chooses to have their children sleep with them and share a bed long-term should realize the dynamics they are creating for the family. Accept that intimacy with your partner will be difficult. Accept that children **do not** automatically one day say they want to be in their own beds. Most children wouldn't choose to separate until puberty. Also, when children are raised with co-sleeping, it is difficult for them to sleep on their own, even in adulthood, thus creating sleep disturbances. If you do love co-sleeping, consider what you want to create for your child's future. Remember, the first three years of life are formative. It may be quite difficult for a child over two years to learn to sleep alone.

The mother who called me had an eighteen-month-old baby. I suggested the following plan: She should start to train William to sleep in the crib by putting him down and sitting next to the crib until he fell asleep. Gradually, over a week, she sat with him less and less time until she was able to just put him in the crib and sit farther away from the crib, then outside the door.

By the second week, William was able to sleep alone and was happier and friendlier. According to Mom, as well as the daycare center where she took him daily while she worked, he was more tolerant of their separation. He even waved bye-bye at naptime and lay down in his crib with a smile! This is a sign of a well-adjusted and well-rested child. When a baby can separate from his parents easily, he truly has learned the art of self-regulation.

Chapter 6: Your Six- to Twelve-Month-Old

Active Time

If I have a favorite age group, this is it. I love these little, active, expressive souls. Babies at six months are learning to use their bodies and like to play games. They are constantly evolving and coming into their true personalities. They are like little sponges, soaking up the world in everything they do and everywhere they explore. Once they learn to move, there is no stopping them. Constant vigilant attention is needed, as they want to investigate every corner of their world. New discoveries bring glee to their faces. At six months and beyond, babies are practicing skills such as sitting, standing, walking, and learning language. Baby's brain is continuing to become fully linked to the rest of his body as he learns to control his physical movements. He learns advanced systems of movement such as rolling the wrist, standing when supported, blinking on purpose, sticking out his tongue, and belly laughing. Baby has also learned to be empathetic, confused, scared, angry, and to manipulate parents to get what he wants.

A strong six-month-old baby can twist and turn and sit up on her own and even crawl well. Nothing is out of reach. Baby must be watched constantly! Even a small dried-up chunk of food left on the floor can be found and turned into a choking object. If you have not yet done so, learn choke-saving techniques and CPR so you are well prepared in case of an emergency. Also, remember to always monitor your child when feeding. This is a good age to encourage baby to sit and eat and not "feed on the run." Small babies breathe quickly and cannot chew, swallow, and inhale air all in rhythm when they are moving and speeding up their breathing rate. So please, follow this safety rule: *No feeding children when they are in motion!* This is an opportunity to teach children to sit while they eat.

Babies in this age group have brains that are developing faster than their bodies. They often become frustrated and impatient when they cannot achieve a simple task. If they can't reach far enough to grab a toy, and don't know how to crawl and move to retrieve it, they complain with loud grunts. They often sound like little cavemen! Their brains say they know how to pick up a toy and bring it to their mouths, but their bodies won't always cooperate. Think how frustrating this must feel to them. They are working hard at linking brain neurons to body nerves and muscles at this age.

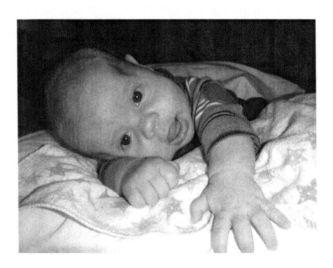

Tummy time is still very important. It is through stretching and moving on the floor and in your arms that baby's small body links messages of movement to his brain and he gains strength and flexibility as well as endurance. Make sure you spend at least a few hours a day with him on the floor, moving around with him and encouraging him to become stronger. You should become his fitness and development coach. Praise him and tell him he can do it! Push him a little beyond his comfort limit. By encouraging him to last a little longer in an activity, you are helping him build frustration tolerance, an essential skill. This will serve him well as he learns more advanced tasks later. Try drumming with your fingers or hands on the floor in front of baby. It is a good way to get him to stay facing the floor and not roll over onto his back. If he does roll over, just roll him back again and keep encouraging him. Weaker babies will want to take the easy route and roll onto their backs, a position of rest, to prevent getting tired from holding their heads up against gravity.

In just a few weeks, as you push them and encourage them to try harder, you will notice quite an improvement in their strength and endurance. Work out at least a few hours a day with your baby, but not all in one session. Some babies can only handle ten minutes at a time; try giving them at least a five-minute break with a five-minute workout. A strong infant will easily stay and play on the floor with toys in front of him for an hour or more. When your baby is able to spend at least a one-hour play session on the floor on his tummy, you have a strong, capable baby. *Good job!*

Water play with your baby can be great fun, whether in the bath or swimming pool. Close supervision is always important around water, so make sure your baby is well supported while in the tub or pool. Teach your baby that water in her face is normal as well as fun. Take a cup and count, "one, two, three," and say, "whoosh." Then pour the water over her head and laugh. Start with a small amount and then use more as she learns to tolerate this form of play. She will quickly learn to hold her breath from your signals and will be fine with water in her face. This kind of water play can make hair and face washing easier for you both as your child grows into the toddler years. When babies don't get this kind of water exposure early in life, they can refuse to put their faces in the water and resist learning to swim later, or fight you when you want to wash their faces and hair. These fights can become quite emotional at two, three, and four years of age. Believe me, I have heard the stories!

Games

Game playing also becomes quite fun in this age group. Learn some games such as "Head, Shoulders, Knees, and Toes" or "This Little Piggy" to sing to your baby. It will allow you to start incorporating language lessons into playtime. Many parents don't believe that their baby comprehends much at this age, but some studies indicate six-month-olds can understand 80 percent of what we say to them. Assume your baby will understand you. Babies often pay more attention to the tone of your voice than to the words. This is how they perceive the feeling of the conversation. As they learn, they will link words to meaning. Be respectful and include your baby in the conversation. Tell your baby what you intend to do, and ask for his cooperation. It is never too early to say, "Mommy needs you to get dressed now, so help me by putting your foot into this leg hole."

Baby Signs

| "Eat" | "More" | "All Done" |

Teaching your baby a few simple hand signs can also help her be less frustrated. It is easier to use the hands to communicate than words at this age. Hunger can be communicated with a pat on the stomach; a wet or a dirty diaper can be communicated with a pat of the hand on the diaper. Your baby will thrive on connecting with you. Helping her to become a good communicator of her needs will help you relate well to each other. Many communities offer classes on "baby signing," or go to your local library for written resources to help you teach her. It can be great fun. Every parent teaches baby to wave "bye-bye" to friends and family. This is a baby sign an eight-month-old can learn. Work on other hand signs and you will be surprised how quickly baby can tell you her needs. It isn't difficult to teach, but it does require consistent reinforcement. Always say the word and sign at the same time so she is learning both.

Since a baby's brain is advancing quickly, use the opportunity to expose him to lots of new things. Talk to him about different textures, smells, sounds, and sights. Begin teaching colors, numbers, directions, and even a foreign language. You will be surprised how much he can remember. I know of babies who could spell simple words by the age of eighteen months and knew all the basic colors. By the age of three, a baby is capable of reading many words and even solving simple math problems and learning new languages. Their brains are craving knowledge and it is important to take advantage of these windows of opportunity when baby is excited and interested. Most parents don't attempt teaching advanced concepts, but if your baby seems interested, don't hesitate. You can find many resources to guide your way.

Teaching should not be a chore but a fun game of exploration. We all differ in intelligence and talent. You will begin to see what experiences your baby enjoys and what objects she likes. Would she prefer physical games like crawl and find, or more mental anticipatory ones like "One, Two, Three, Blow on the Tummy?" Does she love learning to point to new things? How about music? Remember, your baby will probably enjoy learning games earlier in the day and only for short periods of time. Don't make this stressful for either of you. Take frequent breaks. Twenty minutes is a good period of time to spend teaching and playing at this age. After this time, take a ten-minute break, and then try another twenty-minute stretch. Trust your child to show you when she has had enough. Watch for signals of turning away, lack of focus, and rubbing her eyes. This usually means it is time to take a rest or quit. A nap may be needed.

Naps

At six to nine months of age, a baby is often still taking three naps a day. The first nap usually happens one-and-a-half to two hours after awakening from night sleep. Expect the first nap to last about an hour to an hour-and-a-half. The second nap is usually about two to two-and-a-half hours after the first, and it also lasts about an hour. The third nap is about two to two-and-a-half-hours after the second nap. It is usually the most difficult and shortest nap of the day.

Try to make sure your baby doesn't get put down too late in the day for this last nap. If it lasts beyond 4:00 PM, it can interfere with bedtime and a good night's sleep. Try to be consistent in the way you offer your baby naps. Use a good framework and follow the clock. At this age a baby's sleep sessions should be happening at predictable times. Assuming wake-up times and bedtimes are consistent, nap times will also be at pretty much the same time each day.

Giving your baby familiar cues and offering a predictable rhythm around naps will help build good sleep habits and cooperative behavior. When you see your baby lose interest in toys and want more attention from you, or if he wants to be held more, it is often a sign he needs a nap. Don't wait too long to offer a nap or you will end up with a cranky baby. Most babies this age can only last five to ten minutes beyond their moment of readiness for napping before being "over the edge" and then fussy. If you wait until baby is fussing, there will be more crying when you put him down to sleep. A well-rested baby is a happy baby.

Sleep should be getting easier as baby gets more active. Every parent feels differently about the age at which she or he is comfortable letting baby cry before sleep. In my experience, the longer you wait after a baby is six months of age, the harder it is on the parent when it comes to sleep training. Sometimes, babies do resist taking naps. This world of ours is very exciting and they just do not want to shut their eyes and miss anything. You are the caretaker of their sleep, so it is important to not over-schedule your baby's activities. Doing too much (or too little) activity can cause naps to come undone. Although difficult for many active parents, it does become more and more important for you to be at home for your baby's naptime the older she becomes. Many babies just don't sleep well "on the road" or in the stroller. Movement during sleep inhibits sleep cycles from being completed. Noises will tend to make baby wake up too soon. At the end of the day you risk a sleep-deprived baby.

Attachment

As babies get more active, they can also get more and more attached to a caregiver or parent. Attachment is a good thing emotionally. We all need to feel connected, but children can learn to become overly attached and clingy. Most parents do not want this behavior; so if it's *not* your intention to raise a clingy child, start at this age to teach him more independent sleeping skills so he can grow into a more independent child. I hope you have read the previous chapters in this book and have created a good sleeping framework for your baby. While it may take some time, practicing good sleep habits really will pay off in your child's future. Many parents think sleep problems will disappear as a child grows older. Usually, this isn't the case. Bad sleepers in late infancy can become bad sleepers into toddler years, childhood, and then adulthood. Working on sleep issues in infancy is a gift for your child's future.

Baby Sleep Schedule

Example of a Day/Night Rhythm

<u>Six to Twelve Months</u>

The more active your baby, the more she is ready to sleep ten to twelve hours at night without waking. Building strength and learning to roll and crawl will make her ready for this schedule. Remember feedings should be about three to three-and-a-half hours apart. If your baby cannot go that long between feedings most of the time, she may not be ready to sleep through the night.

6:00 AM	Baby awakens. You offer milk shortly thereafter.
6:30 AM	Feeding finished. Change diaper.
7:00 AM	Offer solid foods.
7:30 AM	Playtime—don't forget to include lots of tummy time!
8:00 to 8:30 AM	Baby is tired and needs a nap. Expect one to two hours of sleep. Continue the sleep training you have begun. Put baby in the crib and let her fuss to sleep. Only go in after fifteen to twenty minutes if baby is crying loudly. Reassure her and leave the room. It may take some time, but eventually, as the baby learns

to fall asleep, this time will lessen to about five to ten minutes of fussy behavior.

9 to 10:00 AM   Baby awakens. Offer milk shortly thereafter. Change diaper and have playtime when feeding is finished.

11:00 AM   Offer solid foods.

11:30 AM to 2:00 PM   Playtime.

1:00 or 2:00 PM   Offer a second nap at this time, or about three hours after last nap. Expect about one hour of sleep.

2:00 to 3:00 PM   Baby awakens. Offer milk and snack. Have playtime until about 5:00 PM, when the dinner, bath, and bedtime routine starts. Make sure to follow a sleep routine such as feeding, bathing, dressing for bed, rocking, and cuddling, then into the crib *awake*. Turn lights out, and let baby fuss until he falls asleep. From the time of the last feeding until morning (6:00 AM), if baby awakens, just say, "Shhhh ..." and ask him to go back to sleep. Remember to wait fifteen minutes until you go in if he awakens crying. *Only go into the room if he is loudly crying.* Don't go into the room if the baby is crying in an "on and off" pattern, as this is a sign he is trying to let go and fall asleep himself. Your presence will interrupt his process.

Remember, babies often react to fatigue by being more active (and fussy). If this happens, you've missed your perfect window of timing and baby may need to cry longer to tire herself again. Err on too-early-to-bed versus too-late-to-bed when sleep training. Hang in there. Success will greet you shortly if you have not by now achieved it!

"Tyler" or When Parents Separate

Baby "Tyler" was fifteen months old and the light of his parent's eyes. Ten months after he arrived, they found themselves separated but still wanting what was best for Tyler. They both agreed that he needed to begin sleeping through the night and saw that it was best to begin sleep training. After Daddy moved out of the house, Mommy decided to occasionally bring Tyler to bed with her to keep her company at night, always in response to a middle of the night crying session. Mommy noticed that the baby awakened earlier and earlier to join her in her bed. She feared this was becoming a habit and thus called to seek help. In fact, the reward to Tyler's crying became a cozy night with Mom—not necessarily the behavior to reinforce! Parents often use this disruption in routines to comfort themselves, and believe this makes it easier on their children. Mom may sense the baby misses having Daddy around and feels guilty about it. Unfortunately, parents do not always respond appropriately in these situations. Forgive yourself for your errors, and move on to better habits.

Remember, to raise an independent child, one must start very young in communicating the skills involved in creating independence. Self-regulation (self-soothing) is one of these skills. At fifteen months, a child should be pretty good at self-soothing. If he is not, don't wait another day. Begin teaching your child that some frustration is part of life. To raise an independent child, he should remain in the crib until about the age of three years, and ideally in a separate room from his parents.

During a divorce or separation, it is especially important to give your children lots of love, touch, and reassurance that everything is okay. If the child has to move between two separate homes, it is important that the routine stay intact. Children can be quite flexible when it comes to their beds as long as their rooms appear the same in general. What is most important, however, is the routine of their days and bedtimes. Parents should try to practice similar patterns around bedtime, following the same bath, tooth brushing, books, hugs, and to bed routine at each house. The routine can differ slightly between parents and children will learn and adapt to the differences. Things do not need to be exactly the same. But in general, parents should practice similar end-of-day activities. It is important for each parent to communicate this to the other. Writing things down, initially, can be helpful.

Tyler was confused at first between Daddy's way and Mommy's way, but both parents were consistent with the rules. Once Tyler was put into bed, and goodnights were said, neither returned if Tyler was crying unless it was after fifteen to twenty minutes. They returned only *one time*, to say "Lay down, go to sleep, it is nighty-night time." Tyler persisted in crying hard and loud for an hour the first time Daddy said, "Go to sleep," but eventually, as the routine continued, he began to cry just for five minutes, and then fall asleep. Daddy or Mommy always dressed him for bed in similar clothing, and gave him his love object (a soft puppy) each time they put him down for the night.

In families where both parents remain in one home, it can be helpful to take turns putting children down for bed. This way, a child doesn't get too attached to one parent doing this for them. Both parents can successfully put baby down to sleep should one parent be unable to attend. In families where there is more than one child, take turns and rotate among the children. Mommy doesn't *always* have to be the one to put the youngest child to bed. Infants do very well with Daddy as well.

Chapter 7: Your One- to Three-Year-Old

The One- to Three-Year-Old Child

Celebrating your child's first birthday is monumental. It is truly amazing how much a baby accomplishes in just one year. Just think how it must feel to triple your birth weight and learn to use muscles to produce movement. But that is not all. Language and communication skills are developing and baby learns about emotions and relationships. Sleep is more consolidated and more predictable at this age, and baby is usually down to taking just two naps a day now. Activity happens more and more out of the house and becomes more fun! Showing baby the world outside is a great activity for both parent and child.

I often get asked by parents of one- and two-year-olds, "At what age should baby be moved out of the crib?" I recommend you try to keep your young child in the crib until at least age two-and-a-half, and preferably closer to the age of three. Psychologists have found that until children are closer to age three, they have not developed the ability to stay in one place when asked to do so. They have brains and bodies that just say, "Move, move, move! Explore, go farther and see the world!" If you want an easier transition to the "big bed," keep your child in the crib until about age three to three-and-a-half years old. Once your child is sleeping well and through the night in the crib, and is old enough to make the transition to a toddler bed, start to consider this as an option. Do not think that moving a child to a larger bed will solve any problems. It won't make bedtime easier or more comfortable for your child. Usually, the opposite is true. It will create new challenges. The older a child is when he moves into to his own bed, the more ready he will be emotionally to deal with the new freedom of space. Remember, little feet can wander and find trouble in the middle of the night when parents are sleeping!

For safety reasons, if you choose to put your child in a big bed earlier than age two-and-a-half years, make sure the room's door is closed when she is asleep, and make sure she cannot open it during the night and wander around the house. If you want to use a crib net (crib tent) over the crib to prevent your child from climbing out, install the net (tent-like device) before the child is able to stand up, if possible. If your child gets used to the tent early, it won't be as big an adjustment. Some parents don't feel comfortable with this boundary as they feel they are confining their child. Think of this option as providing her with a roof over her house. You are creating safety and she can enjoy her new little home. It doesn't feel negative to her if you get excited about how wonderful it is to make this new addition to the room. Have fun with the tent before you install it. Put it on the floor so you and your child can play with it. Then, after having fun, say to your child that you will turn her bed into a little house. If you are excited, your child will be too.

Should a young child find freedom early, it means more work and worry for the parent. If you have no way to confine your child to his crib, or to his room, you will be getting up more frequently at night with him. This is what children do. When you offer them a little more space, they take a lot. They are natural little explorers on a mission to see the world. Be prepared!

Children under three years of age are not good at staying put in a big bed with no sides to contain them. Their bodies think, "Move, go farther, go faster, explore!" With this newly-found freedom, it is important to realize that an active child needs help to relax before bedtime. For a toddler, reading a book, taking a bath, listening to soft music, rocking, having a short massage, or other quiet activity can help create a calm environment. I call this transition time. Think of the last thirty minutes before bed as quiet time. No running, tickling, chasing, and no television, please.

From Crib to Bed

When a child is around three years old, parents want to transition their child to a twin bed. By this time, the child is usually ready. This can be a fun evolution and a mark of "graduation" from toddlerhood to childhood. Before moving your child, talk to him and ask if he is ready to be responsible and behave like a big kid. Tell him what your rules are around sleeping in this new bed, what you expect from him when he graduates to the bed. Talk about your experiences and involve him in an appropriate way in choosing the bed, sheets, pillow, etc.

Make sure your child is able to follow simple directions, and be cooperative *before* moving her to a bed. Some parents like to keep the crib in the same room and give their child naps in the bed to start the process. When she is ready, you can then offer nights in the bed. Realize that some young children get so excited about this new freedom that they don't know how to contain their energy, and they may wake up several times at night just to practice getting up and wandering in the larger, newfound space.

Some parents may want to spend the first few nights in the room with their child to help him learn to stay in bed. Role modeling behavior about staying in bed all night can help imprint positive transitions. Your house is not a safe place for a wandering night owl, so make sure you also install a childproof gate on the door to your child's room. Newly found freedom is tempting!

Some parents choose to put the crib mattress on the floor first and then buy the bigger bed when they know their child is ready. You can also experiment by leaving the crib's side railing down, making it easy for your child to climb out. You can put a soft surface (foam padding) on the floor by the crib, just in case of trips and falls while your child is learning to climb out. Make sure your child's room is safe. Put away any noisy or tempting toys. It can be a good idea to set a spill-proof cup by the bedside. Remind your child that you have taken care of all her needs before putting her to bed. This way, she won't constantly ask you for snacks, water, hugs, etc. Set limits around wake-up time in the morning. Remind your child you will come into her room to get her up when it is morning. Suggest that she remember, if she awakens early, that it is not time to get up until you come in. Be good about getting your child to bed *early*. Working with an overly tired child will only make your job more difficult.

It may take some weeks to settle into a good routine, but little by little your child will learn how to stay in bed and sleep well. Remember, you are the boss and you can establish the rules you want for his behavior. Here are some helpful suggestions:

- It is not a good idea for a television set to be in a child's room (watching TV before bed results in poor sleep).

- Keep the room's decor sedate and simple, especially around the bed/sleeping area.

- No nightlights for sleeping. It is okay for a small light to be left on in the hallway or room, but when the child falls asleep, turn it off. Remind her that you will turn the light off for the night. It is okay to leave a small flashlight by your child's bed if she needs light in the night for the bathroom.

- Use the door as a reward technique. Tell your child you will leave the door open if he stays in bed but will shut it if he gets up.

- Gently wake and walk your sleepy child out of her bed to the bathroom just prior to your own bedtime. Tell your toilet-trained child ahead of time that you will be doing this. Catching a young child early in her deep sleep cycle can make it quite easy for her to return to sleep. And, having an empty bladder will help her sleep better. She just may stay dry all night!

- If you have created a good framework for sleep in the first year, this transition should be fairly easy. However, children do test their parents frequently to make sure the rules haven't changed. *Be consistent* in your responses and your child will more easily fall into a good bedtime rhythm.

- Remember to offer your child enough sleep. If you short your child on sleep, it is like depriving him of good nutrition. Sleep is critical to learning and good behavior. You can't make your child sleep in later in the morning, but you can offer an earlier bedtime. Make sure to refer to the research on the sleep needed for your child's age at the end of Chapter 3. Most children over three years old still need ten to twelve hours of sleep every night.

If your child is already in a bed, with the freedom to get up and out of it whenever he chooses, it will be your goal to train him to stay in bed until you say it is time to get up in the morning. Children learn from their parents about when it is time to get up. Parents who teach their children about nighttime and daytime will show them by these cues when it is time to get into and out of bed. For instance, opening the blinds and letting light into the room is a cue that it is daytime. Light is a signal to the brain of energy and strength. It is a wake-up cue. Putting pajamas on at night, after dinner, is a cue that it is bedtime. Talking about the dark and closing the curtains can signal a close to the day. If you are consistent in giving regular cues to your child as an infant, your job will be easier in the toddler years. If you have been inconsistent with the end-of-day cues, this is the place to begin. Establish clear endings and clear beginnings to your child's day. This must happen seven days a week. Create a good, consistent bedtime routine that you can follow every day. It should look something like this: Wash face (or take a bath); brush teeth; put on pajamas; rock and read for ten minutes; say goodnight to parents and toys (put them out of sight if possible); put your child into bed; sing a lullaby while stroking forehead and eyelids; say, "Goodnight, I love you." Leave the room.

If your child continues to follow you up and out of bed in an effort to detain you, say, "No," firmly. Say, "It is bedtime." Return her to her bed. If she continues to get up, say nothing while you take her hand and return her to bed. Do this as many times as it takes. It could be eighty-nine times bouncing up out of bed. You need to be a robot and return her to bed each time. This is hard work, but it really does pay off. Eventually, your child will stay in bed and go to sleep. It may take an hour or longer the first night, but each night will get easier. Persist! Think of this as a game between the two of you, and you must be the winner. As time passes, she will learn to stay in bed without your assistance. After a few weeks, you should have a child who goes to bed more easily, stays in bed, and sleeps well.

Please read the previous chapters in this book to learn about setting up a good sleep pattern. There isn't a big difference working with a baby of four months or a child of one year when it comes to teaching your child healthy sleep cues. Sleep training can take longer for a baby over ten months than for a younger baby, and the parent will probably have a child with a stronger personality to deal with during these adjustments. Young babies learn sleep patterns faster and easier than older babies. So, when working with an older child, be patient and expect more complaints.

Research shows that children who watch television before bed have a harder time falling asleep and staying asleep (as do many adults!). So, please no television the last hour before bedtime.

Children crave their parents' attention (especially when they are tired). They need touch from them and lots of "filling up" emotionally. Especially for working parents, this can be very important time with your young children. They need to feel your presence and sense they are safe. Try not to hurry this time, but plan to spend a good thirty minutes with your child just talking and cuddling with him, building a feeling of contentment between you. Some of this can take place outside the bedroom, but the last ten minutes before putting the child into bed should be spent in his room.

Children will still complain about bedtime on occasion, especially when over-tired. That is only human nature. Keep the guidelines tight, and you will have less testing. Remember, children change with age and they continue to push and test limits. If you are consistent with your response, you won't have a long training path, but a weak-willed parent will continue to have a battle. Your child has great energy for this game. Accept that this is hard work, but the rewards for the whole family are abundant. Children ultimately just want to feel safe, loved, and to know that their lives have routine. Predictability creates a feeling of security. Teach them where the boundaries are and they will cooperate. You will see happy children and, of course, this means happy parents, too.

At around sixteen to eighteen months of age, babies enter a new developmental stage, which I call the stage of "power and control." This is a time when babies are feeling more independent from their parents and decide they want to explore what power they have in the world. They are trying to discover just who is the leader of the pack. This is a very normal stage of development as they begin to learn about themselves compared to others. There will be much testing between parent and child. There will also be testing between your child and other children. It is the job of the parent to teach about boundaries. The world is full of limits and rules; thus making it safe to live here. You must create the same environment for your child. It begins with life inside the womb, then inside the home, and finally it expands to life outside the home. Remember, this is a critical time. The rules and boundaries you establish in the toddler years will set the precedent for the teen years. If you lose your power this early, it will be difficult to regain later. So, put on your suit of armor and keep reminding yourself to be strong and confident. Even if you have to "act" the part, be confident and sure of yourself. Begin teaching your child about which behaviors are acceptable and which are not. If you are struggling with this, please seek professional help to guide you. Ask your child's doctor for some resources in your area. Taking classes and getting emotional support early can help you build a stronger family system. Hiring a parent coach in the early years can be a blessing to your family and your children.

Talk Positively

The way you communicate with a toddler can make a difference in her cooperation and understanding. Using simple and direct language can help get your point across. Don't say, "Please don't climb on the table." Instead, just say, "Off" or "Off the table," as this is direct and easy. Child experts say that toddlers only really hear the last three words you say (due to their busy brains). This means that, in my example above, they hear "On the table," instead of "Please don't climb on the table." So, they think, "Yes, I am on the table." Thus, they do not get off the table. Can you see where this is going? Next time think about how you phrase the directions you give to your toddler. Be brief and direct and use a firm voice.

Use words like "friendly" and "not friendly" to teach your child about behavior. A friend is a good buddy. Talking to them about being "friendly" can help them understand and imprint ideas of good behavior. Catch them being good and say to them, "Sharing toys is friendly," or "Good sharing." Tell them when their behavior is not friendly. For instance, pulling hair hurts and is "Not friendly." They will quickly get your meaning and then you can say things like "Not friendly" when you see unwelcome behavior toward others. When you say the words, "Don't push," the child may stop pushing at that moment, but toddlers don't understand why pushing is bad behavior. They push their cars and strollers. Why can't they push people? But when you use explanatory words like "Not friendly," it gives emotional meaning to the behavior. They learn that pushing people is unfriendly and therefore they can relate to this feeling. "Don't push" is just a request, so they will continue to experiment with this behavior.

Pay attention to how often you catch your child being good, versus how often you tell him "No" or get upset with him. There should be a balance, preferably, more good comments about what you see than bad comments. You thus can reinforce good behavior with your words of praise. Children crave your attention. If the only way they can get attention from you is by being bad, they will continue the bad behavior.

What I am suggesting is not always easy to do. It takes practice and attentiveness.

But I have observed that in as little as twenty-four hours, relationships can change for the better between parents and children. More positive talk will lessen frustration, and more friendly behavior will result.

Toddler Sleep Schedule

Example of a Day/Night Rhythm

<u>One to Three Years</u>

<u>6:00 AM</u>   Child awakens. You offer milk and breakfast
                shortly thereafter.

<u>6:30 to 7:00 AM</u> Feeding finished. Change diaper and dress
                him for the day.

<u>7:00 AM</u>   Playtime—usually quiet play at home.
                Sometimes, around about 7 to 8:00 AM, your
                child might need a nap if she didn't sleep well
                or long enough the night before. If your child
                is under eighteen months, this nap is usually
                still important. If so, tell her "nighty-night"
                and place her in the crib. Usually, if tired,
                she will fall asleep within fifteen minutes and
                sleep one to two hours. Only go in after fifteen
                to twenty minutes if the child is crying *loudly*.
                Don't go in if she is crying off and on. Delay.
                If she is crying *loudly*, go to the doorway and
                say, "Shhhh ... naptime, go to sleep," and
                leave the room. It may take some time, but
                eventually, as the child learns to fall asleep,
                crying time should lessen to about five to ten
                minutes of fussy behavior (on average).

9 to 10:00 AM Child awakens. Offer milk and snack shortly after. When snack time is finished, change diaper and have playtime. Now begins the prime time of the day, so take advantage of this for activity out of the house and learning new skills. If potty training, this is a great time to practice using the potty!

Noon Return home and have lunch followed by a nap. Don't let the child run around and get active. Maintain a quiet mood with books, a lullaby, etc., until the child is put into the crib. Carry child from table to crib so he stays in a quiet mood. His nap should be one to two hours long. If you think your child is not resting long enough, don't get him up if you hear him wake up before one to two hours. Follow the rule of letting him cry fifteen minutes, then tell him to go back to sleep, naptime isn't over. Even if a child is in the crib and not sleeping, keeping him away from stimulation can be restful. Try to stick to keeping him in the crib for the ideal period of his nap (one hour minimum) even if he doesn't fall asleep. When you get him up, open the blinds, smile, and say, "Naptime is over, time to get up!"

1:00 to 2:00 PM Child is up and ready to play. Outside activity is great. An hour outdoors each day can build melatonin, helping your child sleep better at night.

5:00 PM   Dinner, bath, and the bedtime routine start. Make sure to offer a sleep routine such as feeding, bathing, dressing for bed, rocking and cuddling, and then into the crib *awake.* Remember to allow about an hour from dinner and snacks or drinks until bedtime. Sips of water with toothbrushing are all the fluid a child needs if she is well hydrated from dinner and before.

6:00 to 7:00 PM   Bedtime! Remember, eleven to twelve hours of nighttime sleep are needed for children under three years of age.

Turn the lights out, and let your child cry until he falls asleep. Again, follow the fifteen-minute rule. *Go in only once if child is crying loudly.* If crying persists more than forty-five minutes and the child sounds frantic, hysterical, or out of sorts, go in and make physical contact, but do not remove him from the crib unless absolutely necessary. It is better to pull up a chair and sit next to him, touching him through the crib slats, than holding him. If he needs changing, has vomited, needs new sheets, etc., leave him in the crib as you change him or his bed. It is okay to sit by the crib in the dark with him until he falls asleep (no talking or eye contact) if this happens. Try to limit touch to just the first minute or two. Tell him you will sit with him for awhile until he calms down and that you will then leave and go to bed yourself in your bed. When he falls asleep, leave quietly. Talk to him the next morning about what went right, and what behavior you are happy with (delete the negative comments you may want to make).

From this time until morning (6:00 AM), if the child awakens crying, remember to wait fifteen minutes until you go in, then just say, "Shhhh ..." and ask her to go back to sleep. *Only go into the room if she is crying loudly.* Don't go into the room if the child is crying with an "on and off" pattern, as this is a sign she is trying to let go and go to sleep herself. Your presence will interrupt her process of going to sleep.

Remember, children often react to fatigue by being more active (and fussy). If this happens, you've missed your perfect window of timing and your child may need to cry longer to tire again. Err on the too-early-to-bed versus the too-late-to-bed side when sleep training.

"Evan" or Putting a Baby Down Too Late For a Nap

"Evan" was a two-year-old toddler who had very busy mornings outdoors. He was an active child who loved to run and play. Most mornings were spent at the local park. Mom called me to consult about her difficulty putting Evan down for an afternoon nap and also at bedtime. Dad seemed to have an easier time with naptime than mom. But both reported that it took about an hour to get their child to stay in bed and sleep.

I suggested that perhaps a 2:00 PM naptime was too late. It would often be 3:00 PM before Evan fell asleep, and then he wouldn't wake until 4:30 or 5:00 PM. Bedtime was at 7:00 PM, so the parents thought perhaps he fought bedtime because he had only two to three hours of play before bedtime. The parents reported that they put Evan to bed listening to lullaby music. After finding out about how the day's routine looked, when mealtimes were, and what their calming practices were, I suggested that they try putting Evan down for a nap at noon or 1:00 PM at the latest. After all, his morning waking time was 6:00 AM. It is a long stretch to go from 6:00 AM to 2:00 PM without a rest. I also suggested they put him to bed earlier at night, because a two-year-old needs eleven to twelve hours of sleep at night. If he awakens regularly at 6:00 AM, then he should be going to bed by approximately 6:00 to 6:30 PM. Falling asleep usually happens even later than this time. Another suggestion I made was to *not* play music as he fell asleep. I said it was fine to play it while getting Evan ready for bed, but to turn it off when putting him into bed. If music becomes a cue to fall asleep, then he will want (and need) it to fall asleep each time he awakens all night long. Not a healthy sleep habit.

Two days later, I checked in with the family and discovered good news. Evan was falling asleep within fifteen minutes of being put in his bed! The parents said that he seemed to need the quiet and thus appeared calmer and less talkative as he fell asleep. The parents also reported a calmer and friendlier child during his waking hours. They got better cooperation from him at bedtime, too. The earlier sleep time really seemed to help. They also noticed Dad got Evan to bed faster than Mom. So, Dad became the "bedtime routine" parent and Mom got a bit of a break!

Chapter 8: Special Circumstances

Separated or Divorced Parents

On occasion, events in children's lives alter their regular patterns. Illness, relatives visiting, a sick parent, and travel can all create new and irregular rhythms. Accept that nothing remains constant for long periods of time in early childhood. Remind yourself that you cannot always control circumstances that interfere with harmony in life.

I worked with a young couple whose marriage was falling apart and who were separated shortly after the birth of their baby. As the baby grew older, Daddy wanted to have longer and longer visitations with his child. The problem was that Mommy was breastfeeding and didn't want long separations. A breastfeeding child has a difficult time being away from the comfort of his mother unless parents have taught him to also be able to take a bottle or use a cup.

It became obvious to Dad that Mom was not going to give up breastfeeding in the near future. Mom indicated that she did not intend to wean the child even at three years, as she wanted her child in bed next to her all night. She wanted to feel needed and comforted by the presence of her child. However, she was sabotaging Evan's father's right to overnight and longer visitations. Daddy was patient up until his child turned one-and-a-half years old. He then began insisting that he had rights to see his child for longer visits. Trying to convince Mom of this was not easy. In fact, he had to go to court to get a judgment declaring that he could keep his child overnight. He hired me to help his child have an easier time dealing with this split family's differing sleeping plans. This is an example of putting your child in the middle of your differences. It can happen with married couples as well. One person may feel the child should sleep with them; the other wants the child to sleep in a crib in another room. It can divide your affections and cause marital friction. Co-sleeping only works when *all* persons want the experience, but again, pediatricians recommend against it.

Encouraging this older toddler to nurse all night long with Mom but having no nursing option available at Dad's house can potentially cause emotional anxiety in the child. When the courts allow such a child overnight visits with the father, the child can suffer emotional distress in not knowing how to fall asleep and stay asleep without nursing at Mom's breasts. My hope is that loving parents would keep the best interest of their child in mind. These parents, although loving, were also interested in maintaining disharmony. They used selfish behaviors to keep their child dependent for a lot longer than Mother Nature intended.

If you are a parent who has a child who must be away from you for periods of time, it will work best for your child if you foster independent sleeping skills early in life. It is traumatic for a young child to get used to a sleep routine that offers lots of parental presence and involvement if then that parent is not going to be available for periods of time. Working parents who travel for their work and need to be absent occasionally should also consider this.

Children who don't learn to fall asleep independently from their parents often awake in the night and that leads to continuing sleep problems. Parents need to learn to compromise when it comes to decisions about sleep, as well as other parenting practices.

Children must sometimes advance down their developmental path earlier than normal due to unplanned external forces. I know it can be difficult, but always consider the needs of the *whole* family, not just one person, in making decisions that will affect all family members. Seek professional help in making the right choices if you have difficult decisions to make for your family's future.

I Love My Blankie!

Encouraging children to transport blankets and love objects with them from house to house will help them learn to be flexible in their sleeping places. I think the best choice is to teach a baby to sleep in a crib (eventually in her own room if possible) and thus allow the child to learn independent sleep behaviors. I am discussing this subject because it involves creating emotional security for your child. Children fall asleep in a variety of places. If a family travels, a child is exposed to different cribs, beds, rooms, and people. Security objects can offer comfort when the world around them is moving.

Many parents ask me how new circumstances around bedtime that cause crying will affect their child. I, however, wonder what kind of anxiety parents create in their children when they allow a baby to fall asleep in their arms and then disappear when they put her down to bed minutes later. How would you like to be moved in your sleep? How would you like it if you fell asleep with your loving partner and when you woke up your partner had disappeared? A person's instant reaction is anxiety and panic at the disappearance of the partner. I believe this creates harm emotionally. It is more respectful to tell the person or child that you will be leaving her and she will be sleeping alone. Sleep is a process we all handle differently. If you do choose to co-sleep with your child, the best practice for emotional good health is to stay with that child until everyone is awake.

From the time a baby is about four months old, he is aware of the movements of his parent. He is able to perceive a parent's presence and absence. Thus, rocking a small baby to sleep and then putting him down will not have much of an emotional impact. But once a baby is over about four months of age, it becomes important to separate from him *before* he falls asleep in your arms. By this age he does know who you are and he will understand and may panic at your disappearance.

Twins or Multiples

When parents have multiples, it is an increased blessing but also increased work—and increased reward! I find twins and other multiples fascinating. They are usually better at self-soothing and thus become more patient babies from an early age. They learn from day one that the world and their mother and father are to be shared with another or others. Teaching two or more babies how to sleep well and learn to fall asleep independent of their parents is the same process as teaching one baby. Most twins learn to tune each other out and fall asleep whether or not their sibling is crying or making noise. If one baby is crying loudly, often the other can still fall asleep. While they have been known to wake each other up, and babble to each other as they fall asleep, they generally learn to cope with each other just fine. An exception would be a baby who is extra sensitive to noise of any kind. In this case, parents often split their children up into different sleep areas. Then they work on developing a good pattern of sleep with appropriate cues and sleep episodes. When the babies are both sleeping well, you can then try recombining them in the same space, but at opposite corners of the room. It may take some experimentation to find the right balance for your babies, but you will find that separating them is usually a short-term event. The more you create a consistent framework of your sleep periods, the more easily your children will sleep. Make sure all caregivers are on the same plan. There is nothing more confusing to a child than to have different people (like the nanny or grandma) practice different routines at naptime and bedtime.

Relatives and Caregivers

It is wonderful when children can be exposed to a number of loving adults who care for them. In this way a child learns to trust more than just her parents. Others who love your child can be support people for you during your early parenting years. There is nothing like a good friend or relative to bounce ideas off of, or to discuss information about child rearing. Having other experienced adults care for your child gives her an early lesson in being social and getting along with all sorts of different people. This is a gift. I notice that children who have been left in the care of other adults during infancy learn to be more flexible in new situations and able to separate more easily from their parents. They don't cry as much when taken to daycare, or when they enter preschool programs. They are more cooperative in strange situations. They get along with new friends more easily.

Children know who their parents are. Creating a bond with others doesn't mean you lose the strong bond between parent and child. Make sure, when others are involved in taking care of your child, that they know your child's rhythms and routines and will commit to continuing to support the same structure. It is confusing to a child if Grandma and Grandpa let the one year-old sleep in their arms for naps, and at home the baby must go into his crib alone. Again, think of the emotional anxiety that would create for your child. Loving people should commit to do what is best for a child, not what is best for themselves in the moment. Discuss with them the importance of consistency. Ask them to cooperate with your goals. You are the parent and have the right to ask for what you want for yourself and for your child. If your child is in a daycare situation four or more days a week, you should follow the structure the daycare program has set up. Try to give your child meals, activity, and sleep time as they do. Remember, children feel safe and secure when they lead predictable lives with regular meals, play, and sleep sessions.

Travel

Children are usually in different rhythms than normal when traveling. Often they are put to bed later than usual. They can be exposed to more stimulation and take naps in the car or stroller. Sometimes parents have to sleep with their child due to lack of an extra bed or crib. Time changes can put everyone out of sync. Just accept that travel can undo the best plans and sleep routines. What this means for the parent is that when the child returns to her own home, she may have to go through a week of restructuring and re-teaching to get back on the path of her normal and consistent routine. If this happens in your family, pick a day shortly after you return home and start again. Be consistent and hold firm to your ideal rhythm. Yes, expect complaining. It should only take two or three days before you are back on track. Please remember to put your child to bed *earlier* than usual so you don't have to work with an overly tired and cranky child. Remember, you will have better cooperation if your child is not over the edge.

Babies and toddlers do not know it is only 5:30 PM rather than 7:00 PM. They know the time for bed by your routines and cues such as feeding, bathing, and dressing them in their sleep clothes. Take advantage of this "earlier to bed" plan to get rested after your active travels. We all go through readjustment to an old routine, some of us faster than others.

Small Living Spaces

Whether you live in a small one-bedroom apartment in downtown Manhattan, or a petite bungalow on the beach, small dwellings present challenges to large families. Babies who have to share a room with older siblings can present a unique challenge. When combining a baby and toddler in one living space, the only way to be safe is to install a crib tent over the infant's bed. I do not recommend that a baby share a room with older siblings until six months of age or older. A baby needs to be able to control his physical movement to some extent so he will be a safer sleeper. Protect the baby from having things thrown into the crib. I recommend installing a net-like crib tent (one that has netting that goes under the mattress is best) until your baby is at least eighteen months old. It might be a good idea for one parent to sleep on the floor next to baby the first night to ensure all goes well.

If your older child is a lighter sleeper than baby, consider putting baby to bed *first* by at least thirty to sixty minutes. That way the older sibling can have special time alone with his parents and will not have to deal with the crying baby while trying to fall asleep. Sometimes, when I work with families, I suggest moving people around to different sleeping areas. For instance, you can move your toddler into your room for a few nights and put the baby into the crib in the other room first. Then, in a few nights, when baby is sleeping well, add your toddler. Or, Dad can sleep in the room with baby in the crib, and then bring the toddler back on the second night when Daddy returns to the parents' room.

The biggest obstacle in sharing sleep space with others is noise. People make noises while they sleep. The lighter a sleeper you are, the more it will bother you. Make sure you use a sound machine in the room to help block these noises. It may take a few weeks, but we all adjust eventually. Be sure to talk to young children about the changes you are making before actually making them. Be excited about the plan! When you are excited, others will be too.

Siblings and a New Baby

Bringing home a new baby can be exciting for the family. But siblings can often get out of sorts unless they stay in their familiar patterns. The best way to have a happy sibling (no matter what age) is to let her continue her familiar activities and keep the same time schedule. I find that the oldest children usually set the pace of the family. Younger siblings learn to follow along. Make sure you allow at least thirty to sixty minutes each day to spend one-on-one with your older children. They need your attention, too, and need to know they are still in a relationship with you. Your hands might feel full, but you will quickly learn how to juggle the needs of everyone (including yourself). Learn to accept help from friends and family, especially in the early weeks. It's important to let others help you. Remember, it takes a village to raise a child!

Children with Health Concerns

Some children have health issues that will prevent them from sleeping well. Sleep apnea, allergies, chronic illness, autism, etc., can make sleep difficult. Please discuss any health concerns as they relate to sleep patterns with your child's physician before starting any kind of sleep training.

Could Your Child Have a Sleep Disorder?

If you find after reading this material and attempting to establish better sleeping routines for your child that you are not seeing progress, your child may have a medical problem or sleep disorder. Here are some tips that may indicate medical problems associated with sleep. (Remember, medications can affect sleep!):

- Snoring loudly
- Restlessness
- Breathing through the mouth
- Persistent coughing
- Waking every hour
- Looking tired even after a good night's sleep
- Allergies
- Reflux (often indicated by coughing or choking when flat)
- Frequent problems falling asleep (takes more than an hour)
- Sweating profusely while sleeping
- Sleeping in unusual positions
- Wheezing or noisy breathing
- Difficulty waking up after sleep
- Daytime irritability

Please seek the advice of your medical professional if your child has any of the above signs and symptoms.

Postpartum Depression

The latest research indicates that sleep-deprived mothers are at greater risk for postpartum depression. Your sleep is valuable. Teaching your baby to learn how to fall asleep and stay asleep ensures that you will get a good night's sleep as well. Consider this an important priority to keep your whole family mentally healthy and intact. *Be healthy; sleep well!*

"Sam and Sophie" or Handling Two or More at Once

Many blessings to those parents who have twins! I am often asked about how to deal with twins and their sleeping arrangements. It would seem easy for twins to share a crib as long as they are swaddled and wedged into place, but this is not considered safe. Believe it or not, even a four-pound baby can push with his feet and move in circles. I was amazed at one set of twins I recently met. "Sam" and "Sophie" had been home just two days and weighed just four-and-a-half pounds at birth (a boy and a girl). During my visit, the boy baby (Sam) got so worked up crying that he moved up and out of his blankets and next to the head of his sister! If the parents had not checked on him, he might have suffocated her with his body. So, ***please beware:*** Babies shouldn't really share cribs. The safest choice is to put each baby in a separate sleeping place. What about putting both babies in the same room? I am often asked if twins should be separated so they can sleep better. However, most parents like to keep their twins in the same room together. I find that twins do fine together as long as they have the same feeding and sleep rhythms. It is so much easier for the parent to keep two or more babies in the same routine. I got my practice at doing this during the years I worked in the hospital newborn nursery. One night I had nine babies to care for and there was just one nurse! I am proud to say I managed fine and realized in this moment that I had a gift to share with others.

When Sam and Sophie reached one year, this was their afternoon nap situation: In five minutes, Sam was asleep, but Sophie kept protesting and standing up in her crib. Mom would go in and acknowledge hearing her and then leave the room. This went on every fifteen minutes for an hour; still Sophie would not give in and go to sleep.

After a few days, sensitive Sophie was extremely exhausted, but she still protested. Mom got her up after an hour, while her brother slept on for another hour. Sam woke up happy and content, a sign of a well-rested baby. "What should I do about this?" the mother asked. One baby sleeps and the other won't. I told her to experiment putting Sophie down for her nap in a different room. Sure enough, it worked. When separated, Sophie was able to fall asleep in her mother's dark guest room in the portable crib. Maybe it was the darkness, maybe the quiet; maybe she just needed some distance from her brother.

Whatever the reason, sometimes naptimes work best with twins in separate rooms (at least for a training period). The parents reported that nighttime didn't seem to be a problem. Both babies fell asleep quickly and easily.

Usually, when they are older, putting twins back in the same room for naps will work out. Most twins cope with being together in the same room just fine. But always consider the temperament of each child. More sensitive children are often bothered by too much energy around them, as well as light, cold, and other environmental factors.

Within about five days, both children were sleeping well at naptime and the solution was working well.

Chapter 9: Troubleshooting

Commonly Asked Questions

Why does my two-year-old son cry for a half-hour every night when I put him to bed? He only cries for a few minutes with his babysitter.

The relationship between a parent and child is close. Children know how to emotionally connect with their parent, and also how to complain and bother them. The emotional "tension" between parent and child is a good sign that children know how to bond, trust, and love. Make peace with this separation process, as it will probably continue into early childhood. Sometimes children and parents can go through stages of "separation anxiety." Consistency and predictability around bedtime routines as well as an appropriate bedtime will help improve your child's reaction. Be firm and confident when you put your child to bed. Use partners for this process if they have an easier time.

Why won't my three-month-old baby nap more than thirty minutes at a time?

Be sure to give your infant five or ten minutes when you hear him waking up from a nap before rushing in at the thirty-minute mark. Some babies just make noise as they transition to the REM (lighter) sleep cycle but then fall back asleep if given the opportunity. Also, when infants are not yet in control of their movement, they often are only capable of short sleep stretches. It is a sign of their sleep immaturity. I find as children start to sit, roll, and easily position their bodies for comfort, they are more capable of sleeping an hour or more at a time. Be their activity coach. Let them stretch and move their muscles during playtime and you should see this pattern improve.

Why does my newborn want to nurse all the time?

This can be a sign that your baby is not able to consume enough milk at each feeding, or a sign that mother's milk is low in production. Ask yourself if you are extra stressed, eating well, and resting enough. It can also be a sign of reflux or other digestive disorders with your baby. If this lasts more than a day or two, consult a lactation specialist for advice. Sometimes when babies do not gain weight appropriately, they will need formula supplementation. Be especially alert to this if you have ever had any kind of breast surgery, as this can interfere with normal milk production.

Why won't my six-month-old baby sleep six or eight hours straight at night like my sister's baby does?

Every baby is different. Some easily learn to sleep long stretches, while others need a lot of coaching from their parents. Most often, the ability to sleep through the night is related to physical size as well as developmental age. By six months, most healthy babies are able to sleep eight or nine hours at night. Work with a professional to see if you can figure out if your baby is healthy enough to sleep this long at a stretch without feeding or needing to be held.

Why does my baby only take one breast each feeding?

Every woman is different. Some make lots of milk and are over-producers; others struggle to make enough for their babies. Milk production and milk ejection is related to how many ducts and glands a woman has, how much food she eats, how much water she drinks, her quantity of sleep, stress, and other factors. If your baby is growing well, is able to go a few hours between feedings, and is generally content, she is adapting well to your milk production. Some babies are actually less fussy if they drink from just one side with each feeding. Over-feeding can also lead to a fussy baby! Use your intuition to determine your baby's needs. One breast may work for some feedings; at other feedings you may need to offer both breasts, or even supplement with a bottle.

My nine-month-old boy doesn't like solid foods, so I give him more formula. When will he learn to eat?

Many babies do not develop the desire to eat until they are between nine and twelve months old. Keep offering small pieces of food off your plate, and model eating behaviors in front of your baby. Sharing food is interesting to babies. A taste here and a lick there encourages him to have more interest in food. If you start to cut back on the breast milk or formula, and continue to offer finger foods, your infant will continue to move in the right direction. If by age one your child still resists eating more than a teaspoon or two of food a day, then consult with your doctor or a pediatric dietician for help.

My baby hates tummy time so I don't do it much. Am I doing the right thing?

Tummy time is important strength-building exercise. It is a sign of weak muscles when a baby doesn't tolerate much time in new positions. The only way to build strength is to keep practicing. Try holding your baby in your arms as he faces the floor. I find babies tolerate this better than floor time. Try walking around with him in your arms, and looking at interesting things as you hold him in this position. Slowly, as he gains strength, he will start to enjoy floor tummy time more and more. Pound out a beat on the floor in front of baby's face. They love watching your fingers and listening to the sound. I find this to be a good distraction.

My baby had a cold last week and she was sleeping six hours at night. Now she is up every two hours. How do I get her to sleep longer?

Be persistent in retraining your baby back to the old schedule. Our body develops new patterns of sleep when sick. If you want to stretch the amount of sleep at night, for instance, start with a four to six hour stretch first. Don't pick your baby up unless absolutely necessary. If she wakes during this time, give her fifteen minutes, tell her, "Shhhh ... go to sleep." Repeat again in fifteen minutes. Try not to pick her up. Just acknowledge you hear her. Sit by the crib if you need to in order to comfort her, but do not talk to her. Just be a presence in the room. If she cries more loudly when you are sitting by the crib, then it is probably better to be out of the room until she falls asleep. The idea is to go and return, go and return as needed, but not to do anything to help your baby get to sleep. She will get her longer pattern back if you resist the temptation to pick her up, feed her, rock her, or do other pleasant things for her in the middle of the night.

How do I get rid of the pacifier? What age is best to do this?

Many pediatricians advise the best age to eliminate pacifier use is during the normal development of oral exploration. That begins about four to six months of age. When baby learns to use his hands to bring things to his mouth, he can satisfy his own oral needs. Try lessening the use of the pacifier as a first step. Just use it for "emergencies" and sleep. Then, try using it for sleep only, and just when he is being put to bed. Once the pacifier falls out of your baby's mouth, don't reinsert it. Parents tell me it takes two or three days until your baby (and you) seem to not mind its absence.

How do I get my four-month-old baby to take a bottle? She used to take one but lately has refused.

To keep a baby familiar with bottle-feeding, it is important to keep the bottle in her life regularly. Babies are smart and don't always accept non-familiar patterns and practices. To prevent this from happening, start offering one bottle *every day* from two or three weeks of age. If you want to simultaneously breastfeed and bottle-feed, you must introduce the bottle early. Don't wait past the first month. If you skip a few days without using the bottle, your baby might decide she doesn't like the bottle and refuse to take it. Some babies are stubborn and won't take the bottle unless you spend all day not breastfeeding and just offering the bottle. Try these tricks: warm the milk to ninety-nine degrees (body temperature); offer the bottle when baby is half asleep and in the dark; offer the bottle when baby is playing and distracted but not yet really hungry. Try different bottles. Find one that has a short nipple if your nipple is short, or an orthodontic nipple if your nipple is wide. Make sure the bottle is the wide variety (more similar to the breast), not the old-fashioned, skinny ones. Try a fast flowing nipple also. If all else fails, try spoon-feeding breast milk into your baby's mouth, or use a small cup and give sips. If baby is over four months of age and you are returning to work, ask your doctor about starting rice cereal now so your baby will eat an appropriate amount while you are gone. If your baby chooses not to eat for several hours, try not to worry too much. She will usually make up for it at other times when you are home.

Why does my newborn baby cry whenever I put him down in the crib?

Most newborns cry when you put them flat on their backs, especially when just fed. They are uncomfortable when their tummy is full and they are flat. Try using some form of elevation to the head. You'll want at least a four- to six-inch head elevation. You can buy a triangular foam pad made for babies with reflux, or elevate one end of your baby's bed by putting something under the crib legs (please *do not* put anything under the baby's mattress). Also, make sure baby is swaddled well so his hands do not come loose and touch his face. This will keep baby irritated unless he is over four months of age and able to control hand movements.

And, make sure you have burped baby well, or he will not settle. Sometimes this can also be a sign of food intolerance. If you notice your baby is fussy a lot and cries more than two hours in a twenty-four-hour period, than he may have sensitivity to something in his mother's milk. The most common is a dairy product in the nursing mother's diet. But some babies also have problems with caffeine, tomatoes, citrus fruit, wheat, corn, eggs, and certain herbs. The only way to see if this is the problem is to go on an anti-allergy diet, or try a hypoallergenic formula. Talk to your doctor about this if you suspect a problem.

How can I get my baby to burp well? I notice he has a lot of gas.

Most young babies get gas, especially the first few weeks. The best burping position is having baby sit forward into your hand so there is some pressure on the tummy. Make sure to hold baby's head straight and upright. Move the baby side-to-side and pat up and down the back. Then, keep baby upright for at least thirty minutes to ensure the gas can leave. If you prefer holding him over your shoulder to burp, put the baby's arms way over so his tummy is resting on your shoulder. Your shoulder bone should press gently on baby's tummy. Walk around. Hold him upright in this position for several minutes. The motion can make the gas move up and out.

How can I prepare to breastfeed my first baby? I am seven months pregnant and nervous.

The hormones that change during pregnancy prepare your body to produce breast milk to feed your infant. Using a pure lanolin moisturizer such as Lansinoh® on your nipples during the last month can help. But ultimately, how you learn to latch the baby on your nipple will be the key to comfort. Seek help from a lactation specialist in the hospital after your baby is born to ensure that your technique is correct. Ask for a visiting nurse to come to your home the day after you leave the hospital if this is available in your area. New mothers need lots of support!

Is it really unsafe to use bumper pads in the crib? I was told they are unsafe, but I just bought a crib and the bumpers look so cozy and cute.

It is true that the SIDS foundation and safe sleep organizations no longer advise the use of bumper pads in the crib. Many are thick and soft, like pillows. While it can soften the bumps to the head, baby can also entrap her head between and under the pads. I have seen this happen. A baby can stop breathing if she pulls the pad out and it puts pressure on her airway. When you walk away from the crib, having put baby down for sleep, you need to feel she is totally safe and can't in any way get hurt. Remember, large blankets also can endanger babies and are not recommended. Instead, use a footed sleeper or sleep sack made of blanket material to keep baby warm.

How do I help my husband feel comfortable with baby care? He has never been around babies and is nervous because they are so floppy.

Help him practice, encourage him, praise him, and give him some baby assignments like burping. With time, he will learn and feel more comfortable. Don't distance yourself. Make Daddy feel a part of baby's care. Involve him in feeding, and when breastfeeding is well established, pump your milk to put into a bottle so he can feed his child. Encourage him to wear baby in a sling or baby carrier. The close, warm contact is great for both parent and child. This really helps bonding and babies love it.

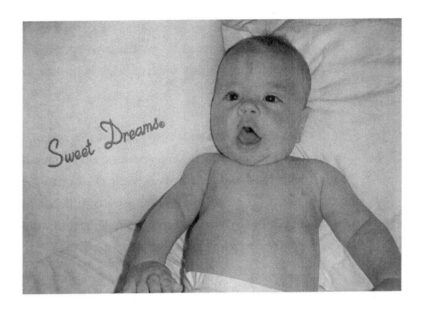

Baby Tips

1. Set up your baby's room by the seventh month of your pregnancy. Babies do come early, so be prepared when the wee one arrives home!

2. Talk to your friends and relatives *before* baby arrives about your needs regarding visiting the first week your baby is home.

3. The day you arrive home with your new baby, take some time to relax and rest before doing anything else. Nourish yourself with food and rest. Rest as often as you can the first few weeks. The first night home is often difficult as new babies can be fussy and hungry, so remember to sleep when the baby sleeps and go to bed early if possible.

4. Print out a photo of your baby and tape it to the front door with a note to any guests who may drop in uninvited. Say on it, "Mom and baby are resting now. Please do not disturb." You can even post some visiting hours.

5. Welcome any food deliveries. If family or friends want to help, say "Yes!" Tell them the best hours to drop by and encourage only those visitors who bring food or other needed items to stop by.

6. Stock your freezer with at least three dinners for the first week home.

7. Have only a one-week supply of newborn diapers on hand at home (for babies up to ten pounds). Babies grow quickly and may need larger diapers the second week (depending on how large your baby is at birth).

8. Instead of using commercial wipes with acid and alcohol preservatives, be gentle to your newborn's skin and use soft paper towels or cotton squares and water. You can make some wipes by wetting paper towels with water and putting them in a zip-lock bag to keep at the changing table.

9. Keep a thermos of warm water near the changing table to use for messy diaper changes so you don't have to run to the sink for water.

10. Use a hair dryer on the lowest setting (not too hot) to dry baby's bottom and also to soothe the baby during diaper changes. Babies love the feel of warm air on their bottoms and also the sound of the white noise. Be careful to keep the hair dryer moving back and forth and keep it at least twelve inches away from your baby so as not to cause her any harm from the heat.

11. Have plenty of cloth diapers on hand to use for clean up jobs at the changing table as well as when burping.

12. If breastfeeding, purchase your breast pump *before* the baby is born, but keep the box sealed until baby is home. That way you can return it to the store if you don't use it. Most women will want to use the pump the first week

baby is home (during engorgement) for relief. Some women need help in pulling their nipple out longer as their breasts get fuller. Having the pump available to you will save you time and frustration.

13. Be sure to start saving some expressed milk and freeze some for future use. Try to always have enough frozen milk on hand for eight feedings (about a day's worth) in case of any emergency that takes you away from your baby.

14. Don't use tight clothing on babies. It makes them fussy. They like room to kick and stretch when they are awake, especially when they are over four months old and it is time to stop swaddling them.

15. Take baby outside (be sure to protect her from direct sunlight) for an hour or more a day to help her adjust to better sleep patterns. The light exposure builds melatonin levels in the body, which can help induce sleep later in the day.

16. Be sure to clean baby's face, eyes, and neck area daily to avoid infections and rashes.

17. Examine all ten fingers and toes every day to be sure no hair has wrapped itself around any of them and cut off circulation.

18. Keep baby upright for thirty minutes after feeding. This helps prevent spit up and also keeps baby more comfortable, preventing reflux from the stomach. If you

must put baby down to sleep after a feeding, consider using an elevated foam wedge in the crib so his head is higher than his stomach when placed flat.

19. If she is fussy, try bending your baby forward from a sitting position with your hands supporting the head so the nose is facing the knees and toes. When the spine is curved, baby relaxes. When baby is stiff, it usually means she has gas pain and this curved position can help move the gas up or out.

20. Babies prefer gentle up and down bouncing to rocking back and forth. Movement should follow the direction the eyelids close.

21. Sit on a big bouncy ball with baby and gently bounce up and down. You can also put baby in a car seat (please remember to strap baby in first) and hold the car seat on top of the big bouncy ball. Gently bounce the car seat up and down. I find this works *all the time* to calm baby down (unless he is hungry).

22. Aim for a three-hour feeding to feeding schedule. I notice that babies tend to eat and sleep better if you can stretch their food intake enough to allow them to go three hours between feedings. ***Do not try this*** if you are a breastfeeding mother with a very tiny baby or have a low milk supply, as your baby may not get enough to eat. If your milk supply is abundant, then your baby should easily be able to go a three-hour stretch from one feeding to the next. Try not to go any longer than three-and-a-half-hours between

feedings during the day. When you do, babies tend to be hungrier at night. Some formula-fed infants can go four hours between feedings, but this is rare.

23. Keep a cloth available at the changing table to cover baby's genitals during diaper changes. Even little girls can squirt long distances!

24. If you notice your baby has dry lips, it's okay to put nipple cream (such as the pure lanolin products) on baby's lips. If her mouth is dry and you notice the soft spot on her head is indented, please consult with your baby's doctor about offering formula or water (as this suggests that breast milk production is low). This can happen the first one to two weeks your baby is home if she is not nursing well or your milk is slow to arrive.

25. Talk to your baby and tell him what you are doing as you care for him. This initiates good communication skills and shows respect.

26. Sing and read to baby during her playtime (awake time).

27. Let other people hold your baby daily. If baby grows up around other adults, he will learn to trust more than just you and have an easier time adapting to situations with new people later.

28. Change your baby *after* every feeding, except at night (see below). Babies usually pee and poop as they feed, or just

after. This will ensure a longer dry diaper and healthier skin.

29. *Do not* change baby's diaper the first four to six hours of your sleep stretch at night. If you keep your baby swaddled and the room quiet and dimly lit, he will return to sleep more easily (and you too!). Diaper changes at night really wake baby up, so limit these if possible. If you must change the diaper during the night, do so halfway through the feeding, then re-swaddle and feed your baby back to sleep quietly, with no talking.

30. Invite your partner to help with all baby tasks. Do not criticize him or her, as it will discourage helping you. It is okay if he or she chooses different clothing for the baby to wear than you would choose. Do not criticize him or her for the way the diaper gets fastened.

31. If you have a little boy, remember when diapering to point the penis down as you place the diaper around him. This helps ensure the diaper will get wet and not the clothing when your baby pees. A snug diaper helps contain urine and stool. If you notice that the diaper is overflowing often, it is time to get the next larger size!

32. Keep blankets off baby when you want her to stay awake (during playtime), and swaddle babies who are under four months old each time you want her to go to sleep. Use a fan or air filter in baby's room for better air circulation. Research shows this can help prevent SIDS.

33. Use a pacifier to help your baby fall asleep if he is under six months of age. But do not keep reinserting it if it falls out.

34. When strangers approach baby (in public) and want to touch him, ask them to only touch your baby's feet. Touching baby's hands can transfer germs there and then later into the mouth.

35. Carry antibacterial wipes to clean baby's hands and feet if exposed to dirt and germs.

36. When baby starts putting hands in mouth (around three to four months of age), clean baby's hands with a wet washcloth each diaper change. This helps keep her healthy. The mucus from baby's mouth attracts germs; so frequent clean-ups can keep her from getting rashes, ear infections, and other illnesses. She will grow up with this hand-washing habit and more readily continue it as she grows up.

37. A pacifier can be useful for settling baby down, but if you can part with it when your baby is between four and six months, you will have an easier future, as your infant will become better at using internal skills for soothing instead of external devices. Babies using pacifiers have more ear infections, so this is another motivator to stop using them early. At six months, baby has good use of his hands and can learn self-settling easily.

38. If you use a pacifier beyond six months, let your baby learn to put it in her own mouth. Hand her the pacifier and show her how. This tool is okay if she is the one in control. When used at sleep time, put a few extras in bed with her, or attach it to a small piece of fabric and show her where to find it in her crib. She must be the master of this tool or you will be running to her all night putting the pacifier back in her mouth.

39. If co-sleeping, consider moving baby to his own crib before his first birthday. It is more difficult for children to adjust to sleeping alone after this time.

40. Put a photo of Mom or Dad by the changing table if she or he is often away at work. Talking about the more absent parent can help your child bond more readily.

41. Make a photo book of relatives. Teach your baby their names. Look at it often so your child will remember them when they visit.

42. At about four to six months of age, hand your baby a small piece of cloth (about eight-inches by eight-inches in size), preferably of lightweight cotton. Rub your body scent and some breast milk onto it and hand it to her as you put her to bed at night. It will remind her of you and can become a cue to nighttime sleep. Make sure to use this only when baby is rolling well and able to move in the crib.

43. Don't use a nightlight of any kind in the sleep area. Light awakens the brain and you want to keep the room dark

and also sedate. For toddlers, it is okay to leave the light on initially if your child is afraid of the dark, but tell him it will go off when you go to bed. If he insists or is anxious, use a very dim and small light that plugs into the wall and does not face his bed, but is at the foot of the bed.

44. For babies with reflux or small tummies, you can switch to a formula that is thickened with rice cereal, or try adding an extra half scoop of powdered formula to their last bottle (in at least four ounces of formula or breast milk). This gives them a more calorie-packed formula and may help them sleep longer. Some infants can get an upset tummy if the formula is not made exactly as directed, so consult your pediatrician before doing this.

45. Make sure any solid foods are offered to baby at least one hour before bedtime so she doesn't suffer gas or digestive distress while sleeping. Research shows that introducing solid foods late in the day can *disrupt* an infant's sleep and not help it, as many believe.

46. Spend at least an hour outside each day, getting exposed to fresh air and light (no direct sun).

47. Do not stimulate baby with active play or loud noises within thirty minutes of bedtime.

48. End the day with a warm bath, quiet music, and a gentle massage. Studies show babies sleep best after this routine.

49. Whisper when you enter your child's room right before bedtime, as you turn lights off, or have a last good night cuddle. A short song or a little rocking before putting your child into the bed or crib helps too. This becomes a cue, so they know it is bedtime or naptime.

50. To give your partner and yourself a good night's rest, alternate shifts with the baby so that you can each get at least a four to six hour stretch of uninterrupted sleep.

51. Avoid postpartum depression by taking care of yourself and staying healthy. Take your vitamins and get rest even in the daytime. If you are sleep deprived, you have a greater risk for postpartum depression. If you have trouble sleeping, seek advice from your doctor.

52. Set limits for having visitors the first month baby is home. Visitors who are welcome are usually people who are "givers," not "takers," and who will be helpful to you, not deplete your energy. Consider that many social visitors can deplete your energy if they stay more than twenty minutes.

53. Ask friends and family for support. People love to feel needed. Let them help you and give to you. Let them walk your dog, do your laundry, or run errands. A community of support people is a true gift to new parents.

54. Don't isolate yourself. Join a new parents group for companionship and to share and learn.

55. Get some exercise by taking a walk outside everyday. Consider investing in a good stroller so baby can join you.

56. Enjoy your time together with your child. *Have some fun together!* Discover new places and open your eyes to her world.

57. Get on the floor and feel what it is like to move like your baby. Mimic his movements. This is not only good exercise, but it enlightens you to his development.

58. Invent games you can play with baby and share them with other family members.

59. Take your vacation when your child is not yet crawling or walking. It will be more difficult to be confined in a car, train, or plane when your baby wants to be in constant motion (after six to nine months).

60. When children are fussy, crying, tired, or ill, hold them close and keep them upright and next to your body (like swaddling). Project your quiet energy to them.

61. Bounce a baby up and down and not sideways for best calming results. Bouncing works better than rocking! Follow the direction of the eyelids closing, which is most relaxing.

62. When transferring baby from your warm arms into her bed, warm the bed first by putting a hot water bottle or

other microwaveable hot pack down on the mattress first. Then, remove it right before putting baby down. That way she won't complain of cold sheets.

63. Keep social and active after the first few weeks of recovery. Try to stay in your normal routines of meeting friends and getting out of the house. This can help keep your mental attitude positive. Take time to fill your own emotional cup daily. And take an hour to yourself, if possible, every day.

Resources

Recommended Organizations

American Academy of Pediatrics

www.AAP.org

La Leche League

www.lalecheleague.org

National Sleep Foundation

www.SleepFoundation.org

SIDS Alliance

www.sidsalliance.com

American Academy of Sleep Medicine

www.sleepeducation.com

Baby Information

www.BabyCenter.com

Probiotics and the Research Study on Infants
www.BioGaia.com

Sleep Apnea
www.sleepapnea.org

Sleep Medicine
www.aasmnet.org

Better Sleep Council
www.bettersleep.ca

Marsha Podd, R.N.
www.GoToSleepBaby.com

Recommended Products

Halo SleepSacks
www.halosleep.com

Sound Machine
www.marpac.com

Baby Bottles
www.thefirstyears.com

Lavender Spray
www.nocooties.com

Lavender Herbal Sleep Stick

www.DrDexter.com

BioGaia Probiotics

www.biogaia.com

Elevated Wedge for Crib

www.DexProducts.com

Baby Safe Feeder

www.babysafefeeder.com

Pacifier

www.mambaby.com

Supreme Snuggle Nest

www.SnuggleNest.com

Lanolin

www.lansinoh.com

Crib Tent

www.totsinmind.com

Swaddle Me Sack

www.kiddopotamus.com

Choosing Baby Signs

1. Choose signs that match your child's interests. Children are more likely to learn signs for things they like and want to communicate about.

2. Choose signs for objects, actions, and describing words. Babies love to sign about objects (nouns) like their toys, animals, and food. They also enjoy signs about things they love to do (verbs), like play, eat, and love. In addition, they appreciate being able to use describing words like hot, cold, big, and little.

3. Choose signs for words your baby can't say yet. Remember, a main goal of teaching signs is to help children communicate when they don't have a way to express themselves with words. Even children who can already say quite a few words will appreciate signs for words that might still be too hard for them—like "kangaroo" or "toothbrush."

4. Choose signs for words your child doesn't say clearly. Sometimes babies use the same sound pattern to mean many things, like "ba" for bottle, ball, blanket, bath, and so on. If your child has a sign to use along with the word, his message will be much clearer!

5. Choose signs that can help in dangerous situations. Hot, hurt, or help can be valuable signs for babies in distressing situations. In fact, we often refer to such signs as "safety" signs. Conceivably, a barefoot baby who steps on hot pavement could use all three!

6. Choose signs that can prevent frustration. Using signs like more, all done, and sleep can help give babies a stronger sense of control during mealtime and bedtime routines. This sense of control helps reduce frustration for babies and parents.

7. Choose signs for frequently-used words. The more often you use a sign, the easier it will be for your baby to learn it. Choosing signs from daily routines like mealtime, bedtime, bath time, and your family routines is a great way to help you and your baby have many chances for signing adventures! Remember, no matter which signs you choose to introduce, be on the lookout for signs your baby may invent all by himself!

Recommended Reading

Brazelton, T. Berry. *Touchpoints.*

Buckingham, Jane. *The Modern Girl's Guide to Motherhood.*

Faber, Adele and Elaine Mazlish. *How to Talk So Kids Will Listen & Listen So Kids Will Talk.*

Ferber, Richard, M.D. *Solve Your Child's Sleep Problems: New, Revised, and Expanded Edition.*

Greenspan, Stanley, M.D. *The Challenging Child.*

Hogg, Tracey, and Melinda Blau. *Secrets of the Baby Whisperer: How to Calm, Connect, and Communicate with Your Baby.*

Karp, Harvey. *The Happiest Baby on the Block: The New Way to Calm Crying and Help Your Newborn Baby Sleep Longer.*

Mindell, Jodi. *Sleeping through the Night: How Infants, Toddlers, and Their Parents Can Get a Good Night's Sleep.*

Pantley, Elizabeth. *The No-Cry Sleep Solution: Gentle Ways to Help Your Baby Sleep through the Night.*

Pantley, Elizabeth. *The No-Cry Sleep Solution for Toddlers and Preschoolers.*

Satter, Ellyn. *Child of Mine: Feeding with Love and Good Sense.*

Sears, William. *Nighttime Parenting: How to Get Your Baby and Child to Sleep.*

Sears, William, Martha Sears, Robert Sears, and James Sears. *The Baby Sleep Book: The Complete Guide to a Good Night's Rest for the Whole Family.*

Tobin, Cathryn, M.D. *The Lull-A-Baby Sleep Plan: Turn any Baby Into a Great Sleeper in 7 Days (or Less!).*

Turecki, Stanley. *The Difficult Child.*

Waldburger, Jennifer, LCSW, and Jill Spivack, LMSW. *The Sleepeasy Solution: The Exhausted Parent's Guide to Getting Your Child to Sleep—from Birth to Age 5.*

Weissbluth, Marc, M.D. *Healthy Sleep Habits, Happy Child: A Step-by-Step Program for a Good Night's Sleep.*

West, Kim, and Joanne Kenen. *Good Night, Sleep Tight: The Sleep Lady's Gentle Guide to Helping Your Child Go to Sleep, Stay Asleep and Wake Up Happy.*

Bibliography

Cheruku, S.R., et al. "Higher Maternal Plasma Docosahexaenoic Acid During Pregnancy is Associated with More Mature Neonatal Sleep-State Patterning," *American Journal of Clinical Nutrition*, Vol. 76, No.3, p.608-613, September 2002.

Coleman-Phox, Kimberly, et al. "Use of a Fan During Sleep and the Risk of Sudden Infant Death Syndrome," *Archives of Pediatrics and Adolescent Medicine*, 2008; 162(10):963-968.

Dorheim, K. "Poor Sleep is Independently Associated with Depression in Postpartum Women." *Sleep*, July 1, 2009 issue.

Douglas, Ann. *Sleep Solutions for Your Baby, Toddler, and Preschooler*. Canada, 2006.

Field, T., et al. "Sleep disturbances in depressed pregnant women and their newborns." *Infant Behavior Development*, 2007; 30:127-33.

Franco, P., et al. "Influence of Swaddling on Sleep and Arousal Characteristics of Healthy Infants." *Pediatrics*, May 2005; 115(5): 1307-11.

Gerard, C., et al. "Spontaneous Arousals in Supine Infants While Swaddled and Unswaddled During Rapid Eye Movement and Quiet Sleep." *Pediatrics*, Vol. 110, No. 6, December 2002, pp. E70.

Henderson, J.J., et al. "Impact of Postnatal Depression on Breastfeeding Duration." *Birth*, 2003; 30:175-180.

Hogg, Tracy. *Secrets of the Baby Whisperer: How to Calm, Connect, and Communicate with your Baby.* New York: Ballantine Books, 2002.

Iglowstein I., et al. "Sleep Duration from Infancy to Adolescence: Reference Values and Generational Trends." *Pediatrics*, 2003; 111(2): 302-307.

L. Kaplan, et al. "Effects of Mothers' Prenatal Psychiatric Status and Postnatal Caregiving on Infant Bio-behavioral Regulation: Can Prenatal Programming Be Modified?" Vol. 84, Issue 4, p. 249-256, July 31, 2007 issue.

Karp, Harvey. *The New The Happiest Baby on the Block Way to Calm Crying and Help Your Newborn Baby Sleep Longer.* New York: Bantam Books, 2003.

Keefe, S. "Link to Obesity." *Advance for Nurses*, January 28, 2008.

Kisilevsky, Barbara, et al. "Effects of Experience on Fetal Voice Recognition." *Psychological Science*, Vol. 14, Issue 3, pg. 220-224. May 2003. http://pss.sagepub.com/content/14/3/220.abstract

Mindell, Jodi A. "Parental Presence at Bedtime may result in Sleep Difficulties," presented at the 2009 Annual Meeting of the Associated Professional Sleep Societies.

Mindell, Jodi A. "Co-Sleeping, Parental Presence, and Sleep in Young Children: A Cross-Cultural Perspective." Abstract ID 0243, June 10, 2009.

Nugent, Karen. "A Doula Makes the Difference." *Mothering Magazine*, March-April 1998. *Study cited in "The Doula" by Klaus in *Childbirth Instructor Magazine*, Spring 1995.

Pantley, Elizabeth. *The No Cry Sleep Solution for Toddlers and Preschooler: Gentle Ways to Stop Bedtime Battles and Improve your Child's Sleep.* New York, 2005.

Spruyt, K., et al. "Relationship Between Sleep/Wake Patterns, Temperament and Overall Development in Term Infants Over the First Year of Life." *Early Human Development,* 2008; 84:289-96.

Waldburger, Jennifer and Spicack, Jill. *The Sleepeasy Solution: The Exhausted Parent's Guide to Getting Your Child to Sleep-from Birth to Age 5.* Florida, 2007.

Weissbluth, Marc. *Healthy Sleep Habits, Happy Child.* New York: Ballantine Books, 2003.

Wiley-Blackwell. "Poor Sleep Quality Linked to Postpartum Depression." *ScienceDaily,* Dec. 24, 2008-January 1, 2009. www.sciencedaily.com/releases/2008/12/081210122236.htm

"Infant Vision: Birth to 24 Months of Age," American Optometric Association, http://www.aoa.org/x9420.xml

Afterword

PARENTS OFTEN THINK THEY MUST have the most difficult baby on the planet and that is why they struggle. However, I have not met any baby yet whose problem I couldn't figure out. Sometimes it is under-feeding, sometimes over-feeding, lack of sleep, erratic schedules, or anxious mothers. Know that these problems are very correctable with awareness and patience. Each chapter ends with just such a story to illustrate a real-life solution I have devised for an actual family. Yours may be the same or different, but rest assured that the solution exists and I would be happy to help you find it.

If the material in this book is educational but not specific enough for your situation, or if you feel you just need more emotional support and instruction, please call me to arrange a personal consultation. When I work with families, I take a detailed history and personalize my sleep plan to your individual needs. Whether you breastfeed, have twins, or live in an extended family, I can help create a specific plan to meet your family's needs. I will never recommend doing anything that goes against your intuition or your family's culture or dynamics. You can reach me in Novato, California by calling my home office at (415) 883-4442. Online

I can be reached by e-mail at MarshaPodd@aol.com. Look at my Web site, www.GoToSleepBaby.com.

I have helped hundreds of families become healthier and happier. Here are comments from some of them:

It has been two weeks and our lives are once again full of sleep! Jake is happily sleeping at least twelve hours at night now. Thank you!

B.B., Petaluma, CA

We got off to a great start when we brought our newborn home. At two months of age she slept through the night six to eight hours! Thanks to Marsha, we are happy parents.

Dr. Mita Das and Dr. E.N. Mayoraz, Cupertino, CA

Isabelle is sleeping like a champ now, twelve to fourteen hours a night. The sleep consult was the best money I've ever spent.

C.G., Enid, OK

I saw immediate results after my consultation with Marsha. Jeremy (two years old) went down for his nap without a fuss.

E. H., Greenbrae, CA

Christopher smiles and waves bye-bye to me now when I put him down for a nap. My daycare center staff says his play is friendlier, and he is happier.

Jackie King, Springfield, FL

Index

9 781450 261647